CW00835599

Twenty-Five Years with T. Lobsang Rampa

by

Sheelagh Rouse

I wish to thank Karen Mutton, the author of
"T. Lobsang Rampa, New Age Trailblazer,"
for the generous encouragement and assistance
she gave me in publishing this book.

I also wish to thank my friend and neighbour,
Britt Permien, who designed the cover,
attended to layout and all those intricacies
of technology and business
which are beyond my ken.

To the memory of T. Lobsang Rampa
semper ad lucem

He who knows not and knows not that he know not
he is a fool, shun him.
He who knows not and knows that he knows not
he is teachable, teach him.
He who knows and knows that he knows
he is wise, follow him.

ISBN 978-1-4116-7432-5

AUTHOR'S FOREWORD

In the sixties and seventies Lobsang Rampa was almost a household name, yet few knew or had even met him. He was known as an esoteric and metaphysical writer, but his identity was a matter of conjecture and dispute as was the subject matter of his books. I lived with Dr. Rampa for twenty-five years, and worked closely and intimately with him. I believe I am the only person alive who knew him well.

Not wanting to attempt what even a skilled biographer would find a daunting task–write his biography–I have written my own story of those years I spent with him, focussing on the early years which were the most eventful. His abilities and outlook were too complex and too far beyond the range of what we regard as normal for anyone to be able to analyse him.

The story is based on fact but some names are changed, events may be out of sequence and in some cases I have created fictional personalities and ambiences. Nevertheless, in all I have, to the best of my ability, painted as true a portrait of Lobsang Rampa as I was able to understand it. I intend my humble effort as a tribute to him.

Because I believe in reading for pleasure quite as much as for edification, I hope the Reader will enjoy.

Vancouver, 2006

CHAPTER ONE

London, 1955. Even now, fifty years or so later, I remember that day quite clearly. There was a heatwave at the time, oppressive, sticky, exhausting weather, it made us all feel irritable and heavy. I recall awakening that morning with a feeling that something unusual was about to happen, but I had no idea then that the day was to mark a turning point, a startling new direction to my young life. Often we cannot pinpoint precisely when such-and-such a change was actually initiated, but in my mind's eye, and looking back over the years, this was unquestionably the day.

As I turned over, I half opened one eye, feigning sleep. I could hear my husband, John, rummaging around, making agitated, impatient noises, opening and shutting, rustling, pulling out and rearranging. I could see him beside his chest-of-drawers, a massive piece of furniture, Victorian and unappealing to me, but nevertheless undeniably useful and well constructed, capable of housing all his dress needs.

John was a tall well-built man, immaculate as a rule and reminiscent of those advertisements one saw of the typical English gentleman ready to board a BOAC plane, smoke a particularly good brand of cigar, or down an expensive Scotch whisky. At this moment, though, I could tell, despite the fact that he had his back towards me, that he was irritated and out of sorts. His reddish hair was standing up at the crown, jutting out around his ears, even his usually compliant striped pyjamas were wrinkled and awry. He was in a poor mood and it was not only the weather, it was something much worse. With a jolt I was shaken out of the comfort of sleep and into the reality of wakefulness. I knew exactly what it was he was searching for – worse, I knew he would not find it.

"Darling, where the hell are my collars? The box has completely disappeared. Don't tell me that idiot woman you employ has been at my drawers, damn it." John's voice confirmed my fears, he was in a really poor mood. How to explain that I had discovered Jarvis, our four year old, in the garden chortling with delight as he floated seven stiff white collars in a sea of muddy grey water, the leather box submerged and, to my horror as he proudly brought it out and opened it, containing three fat worms? "Worm submarine," he had told me gravely, but with a twinkle in his eye. His father would hardly be amused.

Chester the old bulldog, a present from my father years ago, landed with a thump on the bed and nosed up to me, snuffly and somewhat smelly. He was a comfort, an ally in difficult moments and his solid brown body was a reassurance. What about a soft collar shirt and tie, dare I suggest it? Or even a cravat. No, of course not, no one in the City wore soft collar shirts with bowlers, rolled umbrellas and dark suits. It would have to be yesterday's collar. Thank God tomorrow was Saturday, that would give time for the return of the collars from the laundry for Monday.

I eased Chester off the bed and wondered why bulldogs were so stubborn. Never mind, we loved the old fellow and he was wonderful with the children in spite of that silly George, our Scottish GP, in his professional doctor manner, getting so annoyed that I allowed him close to the children when they were babies, and even now would never touch the dog. Did he think dogs were unclean, or something? Still, he was a good doctor, one of the best. I refused to have a National Health doctor, quite a new thing then, feeling that if we could pay we should. Besides, the National Health doctors were overworked and could not give proper attention. It was a bone of contention between my husband and myself, one of a number of similar bones.

"Look, John you'll have to wear yesterday's collar. I'll find the collar box for Monday." I pushed my feet into the deep red silk mules beside the bed, and headed for the bathroom. Stupid man, fussing about a collar, it must be the heat getting at him. Who cares about collars, anyhow, only stuffy city gents. Curse them all, may they rot in hell. I was disgruntled, the more so because Jarvis was such a handful and I adored him. He was constantly up to something new and ingenious. The way he had thought of making a boat out of the collar box, and not just an ordinary boat, but a submarine especially for worms. Heaven only knows how he got the box out of the chest-of-drawers; they were heavy drawers to open and often kept locked. Fenella, our daughter, was different, a handful in a more subtle way, probably because she was a girl and the elder by eighteen months.

The bathroom was the palest green with darker green fittings, restful, a place where one could allow the trivialities of the world to go down the drain. The trouble was that I had not yet mastered the art, and I remember thinking that it was unlikely that John had either. If he had, would he be worrying about his wretched collars? No, he wouldn't. I drew a tepid bath and shook a few drops of my Worth essence into it while sitting on the edge of the bathtub and reflecting. As I write I can almost smell again the perfume, so delicate yet so exotic, as it rose in the imperceptible steam of a cool bath. I even recall hearing the children that morning, already awake in their rooms above, Jarvis agitating to be up and about and Fenella, in her little mother role, telling him he would just have to wait, and in the meantime she would show him her new picture book.

They were both fair haired, blue eyed children, but whereas Fenella was destined to be long and thin, was highly strung yet responsible beyond her years, Jarvis was round, mischievous and relatively uncomplicated. In a few minutes Mrs. Wood would arrive from the flat at the bottom of the garden, and get them up ready for breakfast. She had seemed a homely enough soul when I interviewed her for the job as general help, and it was bothersome that John was so difficult about her. Admittedly she was a bit bonkers when it came down to it. Look at the goldfish, the dog with one lop-ear and the mangy cat, not to mention the daughter who never went to school which meant the school inspector was constantly on the doorstep. But on the other hand, she was kind and willing with the children, and that was something.

Since the war ended it was difficult to balance the servant problem, and I was thankful to have a helper installed in a separate flat over the garage. Perhaps John was right, there was something a little strange about the woman. With hindsight I see now that she was a stepping stone in a sense, but in the present, in the moment, we see nothing clearly. It is only when we look back that the pieces fall into place and form a picture which is comprehensible, like a jigsaw puzzle, or one of those delightful magic paintings that children used to do, and perhaps still do for all I know, where the picture forms as the child wets the paper with a brush.

I shrugged off my nightgown, leaving it to puddle on the marble floor, and stepped into the warm, scented water. The morning bath was my luxury of the day. No one disturbed me. I would lie there and review what I had to do each day and steel myself in readiness. That was how I got through it, got through each day. This particular day, and I remember it so well, as I say, because of the events, or the one event, which turned out to be quite momentous, we were invited by a young man, David whose surname, oddly enough, completely escapes me but who worked in John's firm, to go to a recently opened show at Drury Lane (or was it the Coliseum?) 'Porgy and Bess,' and then to dine late at Prunier's. I adored Prunier's, but knew I would be preoccupied all the evening wondering if Mrs. Wood was taking care of the children, if Jarvis would have an asthma attack, or some other dire emergency would happen. And then there was my own problem with hay fever and headaches, not to mention this horrible heat wave to contend with. David and some other guests of his were coming for drinks before the theatre so I should get fresh flowers, although David always brought exquisite bouquets from Moyses Stevens. He was such a civilized young man.

I heard John on the landing outside the bathroom door calling Chester. Thank goodness, I thought, he must have decided he could, after all, wear yesterday's collar. He always took Chester for a short walk first thing in the morning, usually up to Kensington Gardens which was almost on our doorstep. The real reason for the early walk was that John was quite paranoid about dear Chester defiling his garden. The little garden was his special thing, and I have to admit that he made an excellent job of it. Gardening in London was not easy, but ours always looked quite enchanting due entirely to John's ceaseless effort. We even had things like roses and sweet peas.

Maliciously, I often was tempted to find him an oversized magnifying glass so he could minutely examine his beloved plants for any sign of impurity left by Chester when I was supposed to be keeping him off the garden.

Anyway, there I was lying in the deliciously scented bath mentally ticking off all I had to do that day. Looking back, it all seems ridiculously insignificant, but then it was quite different. In my mind it was vital and there was no room for failure. Get the flowers, run round to Mac Fisheries for smoked salmon, get something for lunch with the children, get my hair set, that would take at least an hour and there was no putting it off, not in this humid weather making my fine hair limp as a rag. Oh yes, I had to ring up the dressmaker about next week's cocktail party at the Trench's. I would have to have a fitting tomorrow or the silk suit would not be ready in time. All that to cram in with my usual day with the children and Chester. And I must try to get a ten minute nap so I would last out the night without hay fever and headaches. As I attempted to arrange it in my mind without panic setting in, I heard Mrs. Wood's heavy step on the stairs, and knew the children would be down and ready for breakfast in fifteen minutes or so. I must make an effort, leave the peace of the bath, towel myself dry, go through to dress. I thought of the milkman telling John that I could be seen dressing from the street, and John telling me in his humourless way, sort of critical and disapproving. So what about it? What a prissy lot! They did not have to watch, after all. There might be dozens of different kinds of human bodies to study, not just two. How idiotic. But it was such an issue with John I took care to keep the curtains drawn which annoyed me because I felt I had to do it to comply with convention, and convention was another of those bones of contention, bones which were so picked over you would think they would be completely dry by this time and ready to break up, but they were not, they kept on being picked, and picked, and picked relentlessly.

By midmorning the thermometer had crept up and the heavy, thick air hung stagnant and ominous. I thought fleetingly of poor old John in the city with his stiff collar and black suit. No wonder he was so irritable at times. I thought of Jarvis, he could be having a problem with his asthma soon and I would have to see he did not over-exert himself. London was perhaps the worst place for him, but what was it George had said? A sort of mother/son thing, whatever that meant, that caused him to have asthma. A lot of rubbish, no doubt. When he had an attack my whole being was cast into the deepest gloom and panic - what if he died? That was my worst nightmare, the thing I could not face, the thing that was like a sword hanging ready to strike. It coloured my life with fear. He was happy at the moment banging around with something in the nursery, pans from the kitchen cupboard and a wooden spoon.

One of our favourite places to go to was the bandstand in Kensington Gardens, and his current project was bandsmen. Of necessity it was a noisy project and made Chester quite miserable. It would be a blessing when Jarvis turned his attention to something else. Fenella loved the museum in Kensington Palace, and could spend hours there looking at things. It was a small, personal kind of museum and although it bored Jarvis, and Chester, of course, was not allowed in, I encouraged her in her enthusiasm. We were lucky to live so close to Kensington Gardens, and our house was a gem – understated and charming, nothing grand about it, modest early Regency. I loved it, I adored the children, so why were there pools of darkness and fear all the time in my mind? I had no answer, so I just shut it all out and - got on with it, as they say. Maybe everyone did that to a greater or lesser degree then. The war was still not yet just a memory. We all, I think, had learned to be thankful for small mercies, and not to fuss over personal agonies - at least, not out loud.

"Mama, telephone, telephone," Fenella's shrill voice demanded I come, that I stay on track and do those things I had to do. She kept me in line, a mixed blessing. Going through to the drawing room I picked up the receiver.

"Hello, yes, this is Mrs. Rouse speaking. Oh, its you Madam D." It was my dressmaker. " My fitting is tomorrow, isn't it? What, it isn't ready? But it has to be, I absolutely must have it for the Trench's cocktail party next Wednesday - you know that. Lady Trench will be appalled if I turn up in the same old thing yet again, she really will, you know that, Madame D., you know what she's like." This was awful. How could the silk suit not be ready for fitting? It was promised! I pictured my dressmaker at the other end of the line, immaculate in black, tall and sparse, white hair swept into a chignon, no make-up, pearls and gold earrings. Only her feet betrayed a hard early life and a struggle. Such a nice woman, I would love to ask her round for dinner, but it would never do. Her rent in Bruton Street must be exorbitant, being next door to Hartnell would automatically put it up, and goodness knows how many little women she employed in the back stitching their lives away, ruining their eyesight, getting horribly humped shoulders from bending over all day long, not to mention the mannequin who modeled the Paris samples for you. She probably came cheap because she had such thick ankles, odd for a mannequin even though the rest of her was thin and long and elegant. But the cost of it all did not bear thinking of, it truly did not. And then her flat in Dover Street, as well. Perhaps there was a man looking after her. I hoped so.

As these thoughts raced through my mind I tried to get a hold on my anger and disappointment. I should say it did not matter, I could, after all, wear the same old thing next Wednesday. Who was really going to notice except Jessica Trench, and she would be her usual critical self anyway, she always was, but – oh, so charming! Or perhaps there was something else at the back of the wardrobe. Or could I ask Cordelia to lend me something? No, that was impossible - although we were devoted friends we were very different types, she far more glamorous than I, more daring, our clothes were quite dissimilar.

I got a grip on myself and backed down. "Oh well, dear Madame D., don't worry, perhaps the heat will be so intense by then that we'll all be prostrate on the ground and frizzled up." A poor try at humour but the best I could do in the circumstances. I felt the headache coming on, and prayed for the hay fever not to overcome me in this heat, it was so miserable, runny eyes, constant sneezing and general lowness of mood. But what were the children doing? There was an ominous silence I did not like, no bandsmen, no singing or dancing. Then Fenella appeared at the door again, her pale face full of agitation "Mama, he's being naughty again, Jarvis is being naughty. He's swinging on the Hoover!"

The vacuum cleaner was kept in a cupboard under the stairs. It had a large ring on the end of the handle so it could be hung up out of the way, and that was how it was, hung up and moveable so a small person could sit on it and swing. Jarvis had devised a method of opening the cupboard door with a stick, and to actually indulge in such an illicit act and forbidden behaviour filled his young mind with delight. To sit and swing back and forth on the Hoover in the darkness of the under-the-stairs cupboard was superb, amusing, forbidden and glorious. The next moment there was a crash, it seemed to shake the house. Then his howls. Together, Fenella and I ran to his aid. The hook had given way, and the child was lying with blood coursing down his face from a wound in his forehead and into his open, screaming mouth. The drop could not have been more than two or three feet, but he must have banged his head on the jagged edge of the nursery fender, put in the cupboard out of the way until it could be mended. My heart was pounding. All that blood, he could bleed to death! Where was that useless Mrs. Wood? Thank God for Fenella. I was in a panic. "Fenella, get a towel, quick," I shouted as I picked up Jarvis and carried him to the kitchen sink, all the time trying to quieten him, with my heart hammering, to me, even louder than his howls.

Fenella, bless her, appeared in a moment, dragging all the towels she had snatched from the bathroom rails. Soak a towel in cold water, that was the thing, wasn't it, and then press it on the wound hard to try to stop the bleeding. In a minute or two the child quietened down, and I carried him to the telephone. I sat down, cradling him in my lap while I dialed George's number. His consulting rooms were in Harley Street, usually known as the domain of specialists, but there was actually the odd GP there and he happened to be one of them. I knew the telephone would ring straight through to him because as well as being our doctor he was our friend and we used his private number. All the time Fenella was hopping from one foot to the other, concerned, and with a kind of excitement that came over her in stressful moments. She always absorbed my own fear, unfounded though it was. She did not understand it, and it wound round her like a great ever-thickened cord that tied her in knots. Poor Fenella, she should have been born to a calmer, more down-to-earth woman.

George answered the telephone at the second ring. He probably had a patient in the big chair across from him who would be staring into space, pretending not to listen to his conversation. But I was beyond caring.

Although normally polite, at this moment all I could think of was Jarvis. "Look, George, it's Sheelagh. You must come immediately. Jarvis has fallen and severely cut his head, there's blood everywhere, but everywhere. What's that - patients waiting - well they'll just have to wait, this is urgent, he may die, he just may die if you don't come immediately." My voice trembled, I had to bang down the receiver for fear of bursting into tears. But I knew he would come, he had never let us down.

At last it was over, Jarvis was lightly sedated and lain in his bed, his head stitched and cleansed, and he slept the deep peaceful sleep of the young. After George left, Fenella was put to rest on the drawing room sofa. We had not bothered with lunch, my hair would have to hang limp, there was no time for the hairdresser, and there would be no flowers except those David might bring. The day was not shaping up to my well devised plan, and it seemed to be getting hotter all the time. Chester would be really suffering, I thought, with his pushed back nose and the difficulty he had in breathing

Chester? Where was he? No sign of the old fellow.

Odd, I thought, he is usually around helping in his own way. Oh well, he'll be somewhere. I placed a handkerchief soaked in eau-de-cologne on my brow and closed my eyes. My head was throbbing, it had to get better before John came home. But where was Chester? I got up and called him. No response. Nowhere to be seen. I went out to the garden. He may have gone up to see Mrs. Wood who, I was convinced, gave him food he was not allowed to have. I could ask her to go round to Queensway to buy smoked salmon and lemons, it occurred to me as I made my way down the narrow crazy-paved garden path to her flat. It was so pretty with thyme and tiny blue star creeper, and here and there moss interspersed between the stones. Little did I know, and I could never have guessed, that when my feet traversed that same path back to the house something quite extraordinary would have happened, something that was to make me forever apart from all I had known, from friends and family even.

I opened the garage door, and as I mounted the stairs to Mrs. Wood's flat I seemed to hear voices. She must have a visitor, I thought, but I needed to find Chester, so I knocked on the door and waited. The voices inside ceased, and the door was opened. Mrs. Wood appeared, but as I looked past her to the figure of a man seated beside the window she faded into insignificance. I knew nothing about vibrations, auras and the like, but such power radiated from this person that I had the distinct feeling of a fire burning brightly. I was awed. My eyes were drawn to and met his, which were somehow long and narrow, piercing without being large, calm and still with a hint of amusement in them. Although he remained seated, my impression was of a short, stocky man with a shaven head and wearing a greying beard. His expression was unreadable. He wore a black suit with a pink shirt and black bow tie. All this I took in in a matter of seconds. He was unusual. I had never encountered anyone with such a presence.

What happened next was at the time completely inexplicable to me, but since then I have read of similar cases; only a few weeks ago I read an account by Sybille Bedford of a person's first meeting with a psychic in which she mentions the feeling of receiving an electric shock. As this man looked at me, I experienced something utterly strange. I felt his eyes boring into my very soul, into the being, the self I did not expose, almost did not know or recognize so used was I to covering up, to pretending, to denying. It was as though I was standing there with my soul stark naked, no pretense, no protection. I had never experienced anything like it before, and never have since. Then I became aware of an awesome tingling all over my body, as though I indeed was receiving an enormous electric shock, and I seemed to be looking at myself from a distance, from above, and I was aware, did not actually hear, but was aware of the knowledge that this was momentous for me, this was a unique chance, take it or leave it. The whole sensation could not have lasted more than a minute perhaps, but a minute can represent a lifetime.

Then the man spoke. "Your dog's too fat," he said. With that he chuckled, rose and stepped past me, down the stairs and out into the mews.

Chester was there. Mrs. Wood was apologizing profusely, she would have brought him back to the house, she was explaining, but her friend had come to catch spiders in the garage for his myna bird, and had stayed for a cup of tea. In answer to my question, she told me he was the Tibetan doctor who rented a room with his wife in the house she had been caretaking in Queensway before coming to us. Dr. Ku'an was his name, a real gentleman, he had done more for her than anyone else in her entire life.

And that was the beginning. From that moment my feet were set on a Path not always easy to travel, but one there is no denying once it has been revealed. Of course, I had no idea then what was ahead of me, or the meaning of any of it. Now, though, an old woman, I can look back and paint a magic picture as I wet my brush and see the colours and shapes appear, it forms a picture which is important only in that it involves a unique and controversial figure who I was to come to know perhaps better than anyone else knew him. Like the sand in a timer I feel my life running out, faster each day. What follows is a story only I can tell, my own story admittedly, but also the portrait of a man I loved and came to esteem beyond all others. I think it has to be told before the sand runs through and the timer is turned because then there will be no one else to tell it.

* * *

That year, 1955, was no different from any other in that the hot summer mercifully gave way to autumn, the days drew in, became shorter and cooler. We lit fires in the grates, pulled across heavy curtains. Autumn in London was wonderful, altogether the best time of year. The London season was over and done with, people had been away, come back and settled down to normalcy. Everything was in its place again. It was autumn. There was a crispness in the air, the children wore sweaters and gloves, Chester was happier and more lively. Fenella was to start school, and it had been agreed that she be enrolled at the Lycee, the French school in London favoured not only by the French but also by most of the foreign diplomatic community. She was excited. I was apprehensive, not about her ability at school but about, in a sense, losing her to the inevitable business of growing up. The eve of her first day at school, after putting the children to bed and dining latish, John and I repaired to the drawing room as usual.

"By the way," John said casually laying aside 'The Times' and as if he were making a comment on the weather, "I've written a letter of introduction to Charles for your Tibetan friend. Perhaps you'd like to give it to him. No doubt you'll see him before I do."

I gazed at him in disbelief. "Charles? Surely not Charles?" In my mind, Charles was a detestable man, no manners whatsoever. Of course he was supposed to be clever and had at least one book to his credit, but that did not excuse him for being such a boor. "Honestly, John, I can't see him being even civil to Dr. Ku'an. Don't you remember how dreadful he was when we met him that time in Sloane Square?"

We had been in the habit, when we lived in Belgravia before Jarvis was born, of quite often dining at the little French restaurant with blue checked tablecloths on the same side of the square as the Royal Court Theatre, I do not recall its name but it is unimportant. The food was delicious and inexpensive, wonderful and nourishing onion soup, terrines, compotes and things like that, and it was there that we had run into Charles one evening. As usual, and not surprisingly given his unpleasant personality, he was alone. He was eating like a pig and indeed resembled one, with food on his waistcoat and dribbles on his plump, unenticing chin. He lacked the courtesy to rise to greet us, almost an insult and certainly uncivilized.

"I think you misjudge him, Sheelagh. He's an intellectual and has his head in the clouds. He may be able to suggest some kind of work at the museum for your friend. He's the only person we know who'd have time for a down-and-out foreigner."

"Down-and-out foreigner? After all, we might be down-and-out if we lived in Tibet!" It seemed to me that John was being nasty quite unnecessarily.

I crossed the room to the drum table which served as my writing table, opened the silver box sitting there and took out a Turkish cigarette. It was a charming old box not intended, actually, for cigarettes – maybe for patches or jewellery - but like most things in our house it was utilized for something quite different from its original purpose. It drove my husband completely insane. No imagination, you see. I lightly tapped the cigarette and placed it in my holder slowly, playing for time. John came over, flicked his lighter and held it for me to light my cigarette. Over the flame I could see his piercingly blue deep-set eyes, which were really quite beautiful, watching me intently.

"Give him the letter, darling. It's the best I can do for the fellow. I don't know what you see in him. Got to be careful of these wogs you know, different code, find yourself in trouble before you know it. Best thing's to give him a wide berth. Let's hope he gets work, it'll get him off our back." He was being nasty, no doubt about it.

I had seen Dr. Ku'an several times in the last few weeks, and I was increasingly fascinated by him. He came often to catch spiders for his myna bird and to see Mrs. Wood who seemed to be his protégé, although it was hard to understand why as, in truth, I had no great opinion of her myself by this time and was beginning to question my wisdom in employing her, although now, so many years later, as I have already said, I understand her importance in my own life. One afternoon, when I came home up the mews and into the garage, there was Dr. Ku'an with his small cardboard box on a spider hunt. We had chatted and he had asked if he might have a few minutes to talk to John.

It was arranged, and he had explained his difficulty in obtaining work as a foreigner who was without the usual credentials. Was John able to suggest anything? So here was John sending him to this man whom I found so uncouth. I suppose it was impressive that he was a curator, or something, at such an important museum but, quite honestly, museums were not especially my thing. All that gazing through glass at displaced objects, wondering what on earth they were, and trying to look intelligent – I found it quite trying. Besides, the floor in those places was hard on the feet. Fenella might like looking at things in an intimate, comfortable museum, but that was quite different. However, I could see that John was not going to do anything more for Dr. Ku'an, so I took the letter and placed it in one of the drum table drawers, resolving to deliver it as soon as possible. As it turned out, I was able to do so the very next day. I stubbed out my cigarette and made my way upstairs to bed, leaving John to take Chester for his final stroll of the evening.

In the morning taking Fenella to school for the first time was a milestone that had to be got past, got over, dealt with. Although she had carefully and painstakingly selected her clothes for her first day at school and we had lain them out in readiness the previous night, by morning she had decided on something quite different. I heard raised voices between her and Mrs. Wood as I took my bath, then Jarvis strumming with his feet on his chair rail as he did when there was trouble of any kind. By the time we had sorted it out we were late with breakfast and had to hustle to get Chester installed in the front seat of my little car and the children in the back together. I remember how Fenella looked every inch a schoolgirl, her golden hair had been newly cut at Harrods and she was wearing a navy and red checked dress, the skirt of which was short and pleated, and navy blue tights. Jarvis was miffed that he was not going to school - whatever that was - also, and he made his displeasure felt by being excessively noisy and singing at the top of his voice. I knew my way around London well enough, and we set off down Kensington Church Street, to Kensington High Street and on to Gloucester Road, then down on to the Boltons, a small treed circle surrounded by large to medium sized Victorian houses. This was a lovely setting for the kindergarten, more homely than the Lycee proper.

"Where we going, Mama?" Jarvis wanted to know, but Fenella shushed him. This was her day and she had no intention of being embarrassed by Jarvis and his silly questions. She wished he did not have sticking plasters on his knees and that horrid scab on his nose from falling off the swings in the playground. He was always doing something awful, and he did not seem to care. It would have been much better to have left him in the car with Chester, she thought. The small, wiry Frenchwoman in charge came to greet us and with typical French charm and perception spoke in English. "Mrs. Rouse, and this must be Fenella. With a beautiful name like that she is going to fit in so well with us. Come along, Fenella, we'll meet the other children "

"Off you go, darling, enjoy yourself and we'll be back for you this afternoon." I smiled at the French woman, "Goodbye, mam'selle, au revoir and thank you."

As I turned away and walked back towards the car with Jarvis grasping my hand with his sticky one, I was in an upset state of mind. I felt bereft. I wondered if all mothers felt like this. I had a nasty feeling that I was going to start sneezing at any moment, but mercifully had had the foresight to take with me one of John's big red handkerchiefs. Chester was patiently waiting, and I put Jarvis in the back seat with the faithful old dog beside him. As we started on our way back up Gloucester Road, I began to wonder how I was going to manage Jarvis alone. As if he knew what I was thinking he began to kick the back of my seat. "Want to go with Nella, want to go, want to go with Nella, want to, want to." His voice took on a whine and the kicking increased. I glanced over my shoulder and could see Chester watching his small charge, his old eyelids were drooping now, he was a good age for a bulldog, and that gave his expression an even sadder appearance, he looked as though all the cares of the world were on his shoulders. That was exactly how I felt, but my shoulders were much more frail than Chester's. If there were a doggy heaven then Chester would be in the front line, first to pass through those gates, pearly or whatever they were supposed to be. Perhaps doggy heaven had different gates, not so grand as humans. Then again, perhaps they were grander because humans on the whole were pretty doubtful, whereas most of the dogs I had known were saints.

"Stop kicking, Jarvis darling, please. We'll see Fenella this afternoon and she'll be able to tell you all about school, and we'll have that lovely chocolate cake for tea. I put smarties on top of the icing, I know how much you like them." There was silence and I guessed he was thinking about the cake and planning some horrible escapade for when we got home.

Waiting at the lights before turning into Kensington High Street, my mind of a sudden brought into focus that word John had used – 'wog.' What did it mean? It was intended to be derogatory, of course, it was used to indicate a person with a dark skin, a particularly unpleasant, despicable foreigner with nothing to commend them, and his using it to describe Dr. Ku'an was stupid. John was what you would call a plodder, liked to get things right no matter how long it took, but in the process he often missed the point. Kept his feet on the ground and his nose, if not exactly to the grindstone, directed firmly downward. He would never hitch his wagon to a star because, purely and simply, he would never see the star.

Dr. Ku'an may be poor but what was wrong with that? He was a gentleman, never mind if he was poor. And, something else – there was an inner strength about him, some hidden depth, some inner peace that could only be possessed through knowing. He was a man who knew, not a man who believed, but a man who knew. I felt that if I were to question him about all those mysteries of life that were so troubling, the reason for our existence and all that sort of thing, I would trust his answers. He knew. It was crystal clear that he knew. Apart from that, I liked him. He was amusing, clever, but straightforward too. I was comfortable with him.

As I turned the car into the garage there seemed to be a commotion going on overhead. I left Jarvis and Chester in the car, and hurried up the stairs to the flat. On the top step I almost slipped and fell in a pool of water, and more was oozing under the door.

"Mrs. Wood, Mrs. Wood, please open the door and tell me what's happening." I knocked loudly, and waited. I could hear the dog barking and feet running around, and when Mrs. Wood finally opened the door I beheld a mess. The place was covered with towels in an attempt to mop up the contents of the fish tank which lay in pieces all over the floor. Alice, the daughter, was standing helplessly with a jam jar and a spoon. In the jar there were two fish swimming round and round, while three or four others were flopping and squirming on the floor, out of water and probably at their last gasp before the dog or cat got them. Mrs. Wood had the cat in her arms and was shouting at Alice to hurry up and put the fish in the jar.

I suspected that Dr. Ku'an had set up the big fish tank, it was the sort of hobby he would approve of for them and would embark them upon, I could see no other reason why they would have such a large and sophisticated tank. My first thought was to get him to come immediately and straighten things out. Obviously Mrs. Wood was in a panic and unable to cope, and the rest of them, the dog, the cat, Alice, were in no better shape. I stepped into the flat. It was dreadful, it smelled bad and looked worse. As I gazed at it I became enraged, the emotional demands of the day, still young, were welling up. This was the last straw, this wretched woman was no more than a slut and was taking advantage of me. Why was she not in the house, anyhow, cleaning and doing something useful to earn her keep?

"This is disgraceful, I cannot and will not allow this. I am asking you to leave within a month, and in the meantime you must get this cleared up and leave the flat as you found it _ immaculate." I was furious. Mrs. Wood gazed at me, unbelieving. Who would have thought it.? But it looked as though I meant it, even she could see that. I turned on my heel, went downstairs, left that awful mess. It was too much, not only the fish tank business but my own stupidity in being taken in by and engaging this woman. Jarvis meekly got out of the car as I opened the door for him and Chester. Both of them knew I was angry and found it was best to behave accordingly. Although unsure of why I was so put out, the possibility that it might be to do with him was seriously disturbing to Jarvis. He could handle being scolded, but the coldness of real anger caused him acute misery. He tried to act as though he was not really there. Maybe it would soon be teatime with chocolate cake and smarties, anything to get back to being the centre of his mother's world. He knew how I hated it when he smeared chocolate over his face, but that would make me notice him, and even if I was cross it was better than losing my attention. He followed me up the garden path and into the back door, watched me set the coffee pot on the Aga, and then ran past, through the dining room and into the comparative safety of the nursery. He could find things to do until I was myself again, and I was in no mood to humour him.

I made strong black coffee and took a small cup with a generous helping of sugar. In the comfort of the drawing room I flopped down on the sofa, legs up and shoes kicked off. I had a fleeting vision, very fleeting, of telephoning John and saying come home, I need you darling, and him taking me in his arms and saying it's all all right, no need to worry, everything will be all right. But, of course, even if I did telephone him it would not be like that. He would be exasperated, impatient. I was meant to manage everything and it was beyond him to understand that I often simply could not. Whenever I did telephone, I would imagine the girl who answered, I could almost smell the milky tea on her breath as her put-on voice announced the name of his firm. I imagined her listening-in, and could almost hear her saying to the rest of them, sitting there in her tight jumper and cheap scent, "Poor Mr. Rouse, wot wiv that neurotic li'l wife of 'is, don't know 'ow he manages 'er, I really don't." They would all love John, everyone did, they would see him as the perfect English gentleman, which he was, tall, good looking, well dressed and always polite. But what about that atrocious dancing class thing he had said he was doing each week, and when I had mentioned it to Cordelia over lunch at the Lansdowne Club, the way she had looked at me. Cordelia, my greatest confidante since we were at finishing school together, Cordelia so sure of herself, so humourous, so sensible and wise to the ways of the world. She was the kind of woman who could trot into Woolworth's and emerge with a plastic handbag which no one would believe could be anything other than Asprey's, simply by the way she carried it.

"Dancing class? John? What nonsense! My dear, surely you don't believe that, do you?" Cordelia had given her deep, throaty laugh. Our coffee had been served, and she helped herself to sugar. "My dear, you are naive, getting married so young without a clue. Never mind, it's better than a mistress. They all do it, you just ignore it, it don't mean a thing to them anyhow." And she had changed the subject, running on about how smart my hat was. "Do you still go to that little woman in Beauchamp Place, she does such lovely hats. Remember the cocktail hat you left in a taxi that time? You know, the feather one." She made a sweeping movement around her face to indicate my beautiful lost feather hat. Of course I remembered it, it was so awful how I lost things all the time. I had removed it because the feather was tickling my nose and making me sneeze, and then completely forgotten it.

After lunch we had walked across Berkeley Square together. It was early spring and a hesitant sun was beginning to warm the ground. "I adore this time of year, don't you?" Cordelia said, then noticing my preoccupation and because we knew each other so well, she took my arm and with a comforting smile said, "Just remember, my dear, it'll save you a lot of that nasty mess heaven knows how often, and it'll save your marriage too. It's just men, that's how they are. Don't take it to heart. But John's a decent type and you shouldn't worry." Her words left me with an aching heart and a feeling like flat champagne. She was always right, and I knew she was in this case too.

There was a rapping at the front door, tap tap, tappity tap. We had a brass frog doorknocker with one leg sort of hanging down as if he were about to leap, and you picked up the leg and banged it on the brass plate. It was old and I loved the sound, not too strident, sometimes one almost did not hear it. I got up, pushed my feet into my shoes and went through the hall, averting my face from the looking glass as I went to open the door.

"Why, Dr. Ku'an, how nice to see you." My pleasure was genuine, but as I greeted him I realized that if Mrs. Wood were no longer there then neither would he be, and that somehow made my heart sink. We went into the drawing room, but he refused my offer to sit down. I waited for him to speak, not knowing how he was going to take my dismissal of Mrs. Wood.

"I must apologize for your housekeeper," he said. "She has had a hard and difficult life, but mainly of her own making. Coming to you was a chance for her. She hasn't managed to take the chance. You are right to dismiss her. Sometimes we only learn life's lessons through hardship, unfortunately most of the time that is the only way we learn, but that's what we are here for, to learn life's lessons. I trust you will find someone better suited before too long. You need the help." As always, he was to the point, direct, without emotion because he was in complete control of himself. He was, in fact, complete as a person, which is probably why one felt so secure in his presence.

I studied his face as he spoke, and thought how thin he was becoming, not healthy looking, pale too. I wondered if he had enough to eat, and there was his wife to feed as well. Even if Charles helped and offered him something, it might not materialize for a while. And I remembered John's letter. I crossed the room to the drum table, opened the drawer where I had put it and handed it to him. "My husband asked me to give you this letter. It's an introduction to a good friend of his. It's possible this man may be able to help. I do hope so." On an impulse I took out my private cheque book and quickly wrote out a cheque. My father, a generous man, had given me five hundred pounds, a good sum of money fifty years ago, for winter clothes. I had plenty from last year, I had no need of new clothes. The Ku'an's probably were without food. As he stood with the letter in his hand, I continued, "Dr. Ku'an, I would be so very pleased and grateful if you will accept this small gift, just to tide you and your wife over until a job comes along." I handed him the cheque, half expecting and dreading a refusal.

He took it without really looking at it, but I somehow knew he was noting and acknowledging the action rather than the money. Then he said, "This will be repaid to you one thousandfold."

Those words have stayed with me all my life. Constantly I am taken care of. I have the knowledge that that is how it will be until the sand finally runs through and my life is over, just because of one small spontaneous action. He put the letter and my cheque in his pocket, and then said, "Please thank your husband, I shall certainly follow through and let you know. Well, now I must go to calm down the fish episode." He smiled, he could see the humour of it all, that was how he managed his problems, being able to see life as a sort of obstacle course. I opened the front door for him. As I watched his stocky figure turn the corner on his way to the mews I had a strange feeling of loneliness. Perhaps he would disappear from my life. But then again, perhaps he would not.

And there was Jarvis waiting for me, pulling my skirt, wanting to be seen and heard, thinking about the chocolate cake and Fenella coming home. I closed the door and turned my attention to him.

Top to bottom:
The Rouse family;
Sheelagh Rouse and daughter Fenella;
Chester

CHAPTER TWO

For years, when I was passionate about watercolour painting, I used an old Derby coffee cup, or can as they are properly called, for paint water. From the mark on the bottom, a rather elaborate 'D' with a sort of anchor through the erect stroke, and from the thickness and creamy whiteness of the unpainted surface, I knew it was made at least a hundred years before the company became Royal Crown Derby. That would be in Derby's first period, so it would be two hundred years, or perhaps two hundred and fifty years, old. I broke the saucer accidentally. I like the shape of it, the small size and the feel of it. I like the design handpainted on it, executed mainly in an unusual burnt orange colour with what you might call highlights of deep purple and touches of gold, somewhat worn off as always happens, the gold wearing off first, I mean, while the other colours retain their original vibrancy.

I am comfortable with old things but have few possessions now. In the bottom of my desk drawer I found two sable brushes. They must have been lying there for years. One is fine and the other much thicker, and although I know one does not require sable brushes for magic painting in which you just have to wet the paper for the picture to appear, nor even brushes of different thicknesses, I took them out to use with my Derby coffee can which is filled with clean water. The finer one I shall use for the details, the smaller shapes of the picture I am about to bring to life, the things I need to contemplate as they appear and the picture unfolds. The thicker brush I shall fill with water and apply to the overall appearance of the painting. But what am I thinking of? It is not that easy. If only it were! This is only a game I am playing in my mind, a figment of my imagination. The painting is within myself - there is actually no need of brushes and water. It is said that a picture is worth a thousand words. The picture in my mind, the magic painting, will take many thousands of words to describe, to bring to life for other people, yet I have an overwhelming urge to do it, to put it in focus after all these years, before it is too late.

Charles. Yes, now I can see clearly that he was an important cog in the wheel of this story, in fact more than that because without him the wheel would never have been set in motion at all. And it is true, as John insisted, that I misjudged him. My value system was flawed at that time, although I can still say with truth that he was sadly lacking in manners, nor did he present a particularly attractive appearance. In addition, he was a trifle too self-centred and unacquainted with the real world. In those days, back in the 50's, I used to avoid intellectual people whenever possible. I mistrusted their posing, their failure to simplify, besides which I found it a quite unnecessary strain to pretend to be following what they were talking about when, in fact, one had not the faintest idea. What I failed to comprehend, and what is perfectly clear to me now, is that it was precisely because of his intellect that Charles was able to appreciate Dr. Ku'an in a way that would have been quite impossible in a man, for example, like John; Charles was above judging a man by the rigid, artificial system so firmly in place among the ruling class. So that day when Dr. Ku'an presented himself at the museum, letter in hand, he was not just brushed off, he was treated with consideration and respect.

It was a grey and gloomy London afternoon. The museum loomed intimidatingly. The particular smell of antiquity mixed with disinfectant, the echo of feet on marble floors, the hushed voices that museums seem to engender, the faces of the attendants so bored and weary, none of it surely could be encouraging to the normal person. However, Dr. Ku'an was completely at home, he knew museums, book shops, back streets, the London docks like the back of his hand. He had walked the streets of London and visited the places of interest for longer than he liked to contemplate. Without work and living in cramped conditions, he spent his days walking, observing, feeling and breathing London and its inhabitants. When he entered the museum he felt familiar, confident and at home. Possibly it was his ease and confidence that caused the young woman at the enquiry desk, in answer to his request, to direct him without preliminaries. Following her instructions, he descended to the lower floor and traversed a number of corridors to eventually arrive at Room 103. Underneath the number, on a black plate in neat gold letters the word 'Curator' was inscribed telling him he was at the right place. He knocked discreetly. After a pause a somewhat high voice responded, "Enter."

It was a largish room lit by fluorescent strips, although on the far wall there was a high window, long and narrow, which seemed to give onto a grey stone wall, and apparently was there merely for ventilation and to admit a minimal amount of light. Under the window were filing cabinets, dark green and battered looking, topped by various objects which would be hard to define, antiquities of one sort and another. The two walls to right and left were seemingly lined with books, floor to ceiling, which appeared to be pushed in and stacked up at random, but instinctively one knew that the owner would have been able to put his finger on any given title at a moment's notice. On the floor there was an enormous and extremely worn Persian rug, which gave the place a feeling of warmth beyond the normal museum office, as if someone lived as much as worked here. The big mahogany desk held the usual necessities - a black telephone, an Underwood typewriter, blotting pad and inkwell, stacks of paper along with more books, piles of them, and magazines, and a somewhat ungainly dictating machine. In addition, it held a large bust, the damaged state of which spoke of its antiquity even to the uninformed, and a collection of varied rocks of different colours and formations. For the rest, the room was furnished reasonably comfortably, but clearly with no thought to impress or please, a man's room with one or two good pieces of furniture, objects valuable to the occupant, and perhaps possessions he had grown up with so easily did they sit.

Dr. Ku'an took his bearings and formed an impression quickly before directing his gaze to the occupant. He was sitting in a black leather swivel chair with its back to the door, and he was in the process of half turning around to see who his visitor might be. Surprised at seeing a stranger, and one who came knocking on his door without, apparently, an appointment he enquired, "Do I know you? I think not."

"My name is Carl Ku'an, and although, as you say, you do not know me I carry a letter of introduction from Mr. Rouse, Mr. John Rouse. I hope you may be able to give me a few moments of your time."

"John Rouse, yes, yes, of course, quite so, quite so. Hmm, well, let me see, won't you sit down." He waved his hand vaguely in the direction of an armchair. Despite himself, Charles was at a loss. He felt strangely disarmed. This was his territory, his kingdom and he was accustomed to being treated with deference. The stranger was perfectly polite, but his manner was somewhat unnerving. It was as though, in some odd way, Charles' very foundations were being shaken, for a fleeting moment it seemed that the firm pedestal upon which he rested so comfortably was being threatened. He half rose and took the letter being proffered him. He looked at the handwriting on the envelope and recognized John's tiny, yet easily decipherable script. A decent chap, John. Charles recalled that he had been engaged for a time to his own younger sister. They lived in the same county and John's mother, a devout Christian woman, had done a lot of good work in the See his father presided over. An introduction from John would be perfectly all right. He reached for his wooden letter opener and slit the envelope. He withdrew the letter, and read it slowly.

"Dear Charles, I would like to introduce Dr. Carl Ku'an, a Tibetan gentleman whom we have known for several months. He is encountering serious difficulty in finding work mainly, I think, because he is highly qualified yet has none of the usual diplomas or certificates here in England. If there is anything you can do or suggest for him I would count it as a personal favour. You will, I feel sure, find him extremely interesting. Best regards, John."

As Charles read the letter, Dr. Ku'an watched him. He did not as a rule use his psychic abilities overtly. It was too hard, and often unpleasant, for him to know what a person was actually thinking. He had no wish to intrude on the lives of others. In this case, however, it was important to approach Charles in a manner to which he would react favourably. Much rested on the outcome of the meeting. He noted that the man before him was physically unprepossessing. He gave the impression of middle-age although one realized he was not yet forty. Clearly, he paid no attention to his appearance, and was completely without vanity. Balding and overweight, he wore a tweed suit which had seen better days, and now looked baggy and out of date. His physical appearance, however, was of no great interest to Dr. Ku'an, it was merely an indication to the workings of his mind, and that was far from uninteresting. From the aura visible around him, Dr. Ku'an was able to deduce that he enjoyed his position, that he felt he had earned it through hard work. The predominant vibration, or colour, his aura emanated was the green of learning. He noted a higher than normal intellect and the wide scope of his interests. It was clear that he was a man alone, someone who did not necessarily fit in with his peers because in most respects he was superior to them. This was all to the good. Neither did he suffer the slightest degree of self-consciousness.

Charles crossed to his desk and laid the letter on the blotting pad. He removed his spectacles and helped himself to a peppermint from a Tavener's tin standing opened on the desk. To offer one to his visitor never crossed his mind, he was far too intent on the contents of the letter. Popping the mint into his mouth, he transferred it with his tongue to his left cheek, that way he could talk while letting it dissolve slowly . "Tibetan," he remarked. "Well, well, that is most interesting, really most interesting. Only last year I was hoping to visit your country, but, unfortunately, it wasn't possible. It is a most difficult country to visit, as you will know, of course. But I have a special interest in flying machines." He had resumed his seat and leaned forward as he spoke with an air of excitement. "Now, tell me, is it true that you use man-lifting kites in your country? I am extremely anxious to know more about this rumour."

At this point of his career Charles was putting much of his own scholarship into words, writing so that others might benefit from his hard, unremitting work. He had already had one book published, a beautifully produced tome written for the elite, for the few who could appreciate him and his studies. After the success of the first book, he was working on a second. It was to be about flying machines and he had done extensive research, he had travelled and interviewed and observed, he had visited libraries and spent hours poring over books and manuscripts, working long into the night sometimes. He enjoyed writing, he enjoyed seeing his work in print and hearing from others of like mind, he felt he belonged to a small group of sensitive, learned people. It was a passion with him, and to actually be confronted by a man from Tibet who might be able to tell him about these so-called man-lifting kites was an extraordinary stroke of luck.

"Man-lifting kites? Most certainly we used them, in fact kite flying was one of the more enjoyable activities in the lamasery. It wasn't something that all lamas indulged in every day of the week, naturally, but I happened to be fortunate enough to become quite skilled in the art." Dr. Ku'an was pleased with the question, with the way the conversation was going. He had loved kite flying in his youth and had excelled at it.

"Really, really, hmm, do go on, this is really fascinating, quite fascinating. Well, well, I can scarcely believe it. So you actually were a lama in your country, is that really so? How fascinating, amazing that you should just walk into my office, what a stroke of luck!" Charles was agog. John as usual had known the right thing to do, had scored a bull's eye in introducing the two men, and, to tell the truth, my only claim to have had a hand in it at all was that without my prodding he would not have lifted a finger, or a pen in this case, to help Dr. Ku'an. John was like that, he always came up with the right thing with no apparent trouble, and rather annoyingly garnered much credit for his cleverness.

"People in the West find it hard to believe in man-lifting kites," Dr. Ku'an continued. "They find it hard to believe in anything to do with my early life, in fact, so I don't talk about it very much. Yes, I was indeed a lama. At the age of seven I entered the Chakpori Lamasery, the school of medicine in Lhasa, after sitting outside for three days and three nights, motionless. Tibet is a hard country, you know, and lamastic life can be extremely hard, so if a boy fails to pass his initial test he is sent home, and much grief and trouble is avoided." It was a fact that he seldom talked about his early life. It was beyond the comprehension of the English people he had met, they seemed to suffer from a racial complacency and distrust of what they saw as foreign, almost as if it were unclean and certainly unsavory. In Charles, however, he recognized an open and interested mind.

"And you did the kite flying at the Chakpori Lamasery, then?" asked Charles.

"Kite flying, of course, yes, but not the man-lifting type," Dr. Ku'an replied. "There was a lamasery a few days journey by pony from Lhasa. It was called Tra Yerpa. It perched, or rather clung, to the side of a mountain. It was curious country there, immense peaks jutted out, rising ever upwards, and great tablelands stretched out from the base of the peaks like terraces. The tablelands were used for man-lifting kite launching because the wind would come up through crevices from ravines far below with such force that a kite could be taken straight up.

"We made the kites ourselves, of course, from spruce wood poles lashed into a box form with wings. The spruce wood came from India, no such wood would grow in Tibet. The kite would be about ten by eight feet and was covered with silk. We made the skids from bamboo. As I said, the wind comes up from the ravines many, many feet below, gushing and roaring with huge force. We relied a lot on ponies in Tibet, you know, sure-footed little animals, and they were hitched to a rope attached to the kite and urged forward at a gallop. When you hit the air current you go straight up. You can see for miles and miles." He paused, it had been another world, another existence altogether. He was glad this man found it interesting, it was a common bond between them, something they shared.

Charles was indeed intensely interested. He felt he could listen to his visitor for hours, but it would have to wait for another day. He had an appointment with his literary agent that afternoon that he could not afford to miss. Pulling a gold hunter pocket watch from his waistcoat pocket he consulted it, and as he did so he was struck with a thought. "My word," he exclaimed, "why don't you write a book? That's it, a book about your life!" He snapped the watch shut and returned it to his pocket, the while fixing Dr. Ku'an with a stare that was challenging in its intensity, and would have intimidated a lesser man.

"A book?! A book about my life!! No, no, that's the last thing I would think of doing. Who would read it?" It was a genuine reaction. Dr. Ku'an was astonished. In his eyes the Western world was spiritually barren, arid, there would be no interest in or understanding of his life and belief. All that mattered in the West, it seemed to him, was money, power, position – material things. The true art of living had been lost, Westerners had turned their backs on things of the spirit. It was sad but, at the same time, he really had no interest in teaching people to be more spiritually aware. That was not what he was in the Western world for. He was interested only in completing the task he had undertaken, the task to make medical men understand that disease is apparent in the aura long before it manifests in the physical body, and that by using sound, for instance, the colours of the aura can be corrected, the vibrations can be normalized and the illness avoided. But the medical community did not even accept the existence of the aura! It was not going to be easy. Groundwork was perhaps all he would be able to do, groundwork for others to take up in time and use. Medicine had taken the wrong path at the turn of the century when Dr. Kilner was researching the human aura and his work had been shelved in favor of X-rays. It was considered too complicated, and perhaps too metaphysical.

Charles regarded his visitor for a moment. He was not accustomed to having his ideas rejected point blank. Normally, in such a situation he would simply shrug, pity the poor fool so bereft of commonsense not to recognize his brilliance, and turn his mind to other things. But his mental appetite was sufficiently wetted that he had no intention of allowing this person to escape his grasp just yet. "Hmm, well, I understand from John Rouse's note that you need employment, and that means one thing, you need to make a living. Well, I'll tell you quite frankly, you won't find employment among other people. Forgive my saying so, but you don't fit the mould any more than I do. No, you will have to create your own employment. Do you need money to live? Do you need an occupation? What exactly is it that brings you to this country, to the Western world? There must be a story there, never mind the details of your youth." He was forthright, outspoken and almost rude.

Many years later, Dr. Ku'an told me that it was at this point that he understood the antipathy I felt, but had not openly expressed, towards Charles. However, he himself was not in the least perturbed, in fact he preferred this type of exchange to that veiled in superficial good manners. He had learned to be extremely cautious of Westerners, but because he knew this man was, in a sense, his last hope he was prepared to be reasonably open with him.

"A story? Yes, I suppose you could say there's a story. The real point of it is that I have work to do, I have specialized research to do. I happen to be unusually clairvoyant. It isn't easy, you know, to be possessed of extrasensory abilities, in many ways it's a curse. But because I can see the human aura, just for one thing, I have taken on a task. Do you follow me?" he asked, pausing to scrutinize his listener. "Yes, I believe you do. As we speak, I can see your aura, I would see it even more clearly if you were unclothed because the clothes you are wearing have their own emanations which somewhat obscure your personal colours, colours which are swirling around you all the time."

He paused again, he knew this was not an everyday subject to his listener, and he had no wish to rush or confuse him. "You ask do I need money to live. My needs are simple as are those of my wife, but, of course, we have to eat and we need shelter. So, to answer your question – I need very little money to live, although I confess I don't enjoy hunger. I need money for my work. I need a lot of money for my work. I am not averse to asking for it because what I am doing will benefit mankind. But people, you know, seldom give freely, they give with strings attached, and I am not interested in that kind of giving. You are correct in saying that I need to work alone, but a book – well, I don't know."

"Have it your own way, then." Charles was suddenly curt, impatient. "I will tell you frankly, though, there is no other way I can assist you. As it happens, I have an appointment with my literary agent at four o'clock this afternoon. It is now twenty-five past three. I am inviting you to accompany me. I believe he could be of help, he could put you on the right track, tell you if my idea is feasible or not." He raised himself heavily from his chair, took another mint and crossed to an ornate cupboard standing behind Dr. Ku'an. Opening the door he took out an old Burberry mackintosh and laid it across his arm. "Cecil Banks is his name, an excellent contact. What about it?"

Dr. Ku'an rose. His face was impassive, it was impossible to know if he was pleased or offended, but with an old world courtesy, in sharp contrast to the manner of the other, he inclined his head and joined his hands in a gesture of agreement, but with no trace of subservience. "I shall be happy to accompany you," he said.

The two men walked back along the corridors to the main entrance, the people they met standing aside to let them pass. Charles seemed not to notice, accepting it as his right. As they passed through the heavy revolving door, the afternoon was still grey and overcast, cheerless. They walked down the wide steps together, pigeons scattering at their coming. Charles hailed a taxi, giving an address in Regent Street, and they sat back in silence, each with his own thoughts. As they rounded Hyde Park Corner, Charles tapped Dr. Ku'an on the knee. "I do hope you will consider this idea, but even if you decide against it for some reason– which I can't help saying would be most shortsighted even so, I would still like you to come to see me again. You have such valuable information, I can't afford to lose it."

When Dr. Ku'an was recounting this day to me some years afterwards, he told me how amused he had felt at such blatant poor manners and price setting. Nevertheless, his appreciation of Charles was sincere and he was repaid in full for his effort.

Banks & Company, Literary Agents' office was situated on an upper floor of a building in Regent Street. Alighting from the taxi they wended their way through the unending throng of people hurrying along the pavement, a mass of humanity all going somewhere, seemingly without a second to lose, heads down, intent. There were surprisingly few loitering looking at shop windows, but there were those as well to be avoided before they entered a sort of arcade with a door in the middle through which they passed. Here it was quiet and dark, their feet echoed on the stone floor as they followed a sign saying 'Lift.' Charles pressed the call button with familiarity and they watched as the ancient cage lift descended from the upper floors, wheezing and creaking as it made its slow appearance. Hardly had it made its final bump of arrival than the metal gate was clanked open by the attendant, maybe even the original attendant at that, so dilapidated and aged he seemed. "'A'ternoon guv'nor," he greeted Charles whom he obviously knew, and just the merest nod of his head to Dr. Ku'an, his withering look saying louder than words, 'bleedin' yeller foreigner wiv 'is beard and shaved 'ed. Pity 'e don't go back where 'e come from.' He put the lift in motion and they made a laboured ascent to the third floor, the attendant whistling softly between his teeth. "Right, 'ere we are," he announced, sliding back the gate, "getchers on the way down, then."

They stepped out onto a red carpeted floor, and had only gone a few yards before reaching a rather imposing door with a discreet brass plate to one side, more like a specialist's consulting rooms than a business undertaking, and leading one to the conclusion that Cecil Banks preferred to be thought of as a professional. Charles entered without knocking and Dr. Ku'an followed. It was a modest and not particularly orderly looking office, one could say almost in need of a good clean, but it was comfortable and not in the least intimidating. A woman of indeterminate age was sitting behind a straight lined desk and she rose as they entered, coming forward to greet them in a friendly but respectful way. "Good afternoon sir, I'll let Mr. Banks know you're here."

Charles parked himself in one of the chairs, indicating that Dr. Ku'an should take the other. "Yes, well thank you, Miss Bartel. Perhaps you could tell him that I've brought along a budding writer for him."

Dr. Ku'an felt extremely uncomfortable. He did not see himself as a budding writer to begin with, but he also dreaded interviews or meetings with more than one stranger at a time because he was almost totally deaf and had to rely on lip reading and thought patterns for conversation. It was difficult with two people unknown to him. I had asked why he kept his deafness so hidden, and his response was that to the average person, 'to be deaf was to be daft,' and one was treated accordingly if known to be deaf. As it turned out he was able to manage quite well in the ensuing interview. He found Cecil Banks amiable, jovial almost. As they were shown into his office by Miss Bartel, he rose with enthusiasm, extending his hand warmly. An elderly man sporting a goatee beard he appeared sophisticated in a nonchalant way, with a yellow silk tie and an impeccably cut suit. Brown suede shoes rounded off the impression of literary, artistic, legal and business acumen all combined in one, and all being necessary for his work.

"My dear fellow, delighted to see you," he exclaimed, as he clasped Charles by the hand. "And I have to tell you, the book is doing well, still selling, a remarkable achievement for any work with a limited, elite audience. And your companion?" he turned to Dr. Ku'an, "A budding writer, I understand. Always interested, don't you know, always interested in new talent. Do sit down, won't you. Cigar?" He offered a box of Havana cigars, both his visitors declining, but he took one himself and proceeded to cut it. Leaning back in his chair he surveyed his client and prospective new client. Charles was introducing Dr Ku'an in, for him, a remarkably enthusiastic manner. "Ku'an?" ruminated Banks, searching his mind. "Chinese maybe? Ah, Tibetan, well how interesting. And your doctorate? Philosophy, perhaps? No? Ah, medicine from Chungking. I see, I see." He was skilled in gleaning information, in summing up and assessing, but in spite of his experience and astuteness he was having difficulty placing Dr. Ku'an in any of his categories.

Charles interrupted, "You have to understand that our friend here is a medical lama trained in Tibet and China. In addition, he has most unusual powers. Now that may be not uncommon there, but here," he turned for a moment addressing Dr. Ku'an, "if you will forgive my saying so – well, here you are most exceptionally uncommon, I believe. Now, Banks," looking back to the agent, "you know that I am not a stupid man, I am in fact, without wishing to appear conceited, quite above average in intelligence."

Cecil nodded gravely, puffing out a cloud of cigar smoke. Yes, he would agree with that. Even if it had not been true he would have agreed. Charles was, after all, his client. His book was doing well, and he was promising another.

"Ku'an is at a loose end just now, isn't that right?" Charles went on, looking at Dr. Ku'an for confirmation. "Yes, well, so I have hit upon the most exciting idea that he should, no, that he MUST, write a book about his life in Tibet." He sat back, puffed with self-importance and pride in disclosing his brainwave.

"I would certainly concur with your idea," said Cecil, "a most excellent idea. Yes, well, of course we will have to have a synopsis first, just to give me an idea of your life, Dr. Ku'an, and who we should approach for publication, all that sort of thing." As he talked his mind raced ahead. He had been in the business a long time, he knew writers, he knew publishers. Too old for active service in the war he had stayed behind in London, sending his wife to the country to their married daughter, and had done his bit firefighting and helping out where he could with the devastation. Unlike many younger men, he had been able to keep his business afloat, albeit it in a minimal way. It had given him a head start over the rest. To his certain knowledge, nothing had been published in the English language about the life of a lama in a lamasery in Tibet actually written firsthand. There were, of course, people who had been to Tibet, scholars, explorers and similar, people who professed familiarity with the country and had written about it, but it was still veiled in mystery because of the impossibility of penetrating the inner life of the lamaseries. He could hardly believe that facing him calmly, sitting in his office on this grey, nondescript London afternoon, was a lama from that culture. Would he be capable of writing? But if not, well never mind, they could always get someone to 'ghost' it. In any event he must, he felt, encourage the idea. Already he was forming a picture of a bestseller in his mind.

"I'm so glad you came to see me," he said, addressing Dr. Ku'an directly. "As a medical man you may have little or no writing experience, but that doesn't matter in the least. Your life appears to be so fascinating. We can always get help with writing if necessary. I would like you, as I say, to let me have a synopsis, a brief overview, of what you have in mind. We can take it from there. I am definitely interested. I would be pleased to act for you." He waited as the other weighed up his words. Despite his being supposedly at a loose end, as Charles had put it, he did not appear too enthused at the prospect of writing. Banks could see he was not going to get an immediate agreement. Perhaps making his private life public was going to be difficult, not everyone wanted to do that.

After a pause, Dr. Ku'an stood up. He felt this was his cue to leave. He knew the other two had business to talk, besides, he himself was exhausted. Sitting on chairs was uncomfortable for any length of time. At home he either sat cross-legged or reclined on his bed, and he had found the afternoon taxing both physically and mentally. "Thank you, Mr. Banks, I will certainly consider the matter," he said. "But, you know," with a slight, almost mischievous smile, "I believe I can write at least as well as any ghost writer you might suggest. The secret of writing, as you will know, is an understanding of human nature. I am thoroughly acquainted with that." He bowed politely, and turning to Charles said, "Believe me, I am most grateful to you. If I can be of any assistance regarding kites or flying antiquated planes, as I did in the China-Japanese war, Mr. Rouse knows how to get in touch with me." He shook hands, and turned to leave. Banks rang for Miss Bartel to show him out.

Once again back down in the street he found the dusk calming. It deadened the eternal din somehow, and obscured the hundreds of hurrying faces, making them depersonalized in a welcoming way. Should he take a bus, he wondered, or could he manage to walk, saving the bus fare and giving himself time to think. He could stop at Lyon's Corner House at Marble Arch and get something to eat, perhaps a frozen steak and kidney pie they could put in the oven when he got back to the rooming house where he and his wife lived. He wondered what sort of mood Ra'ab, his wife, would be in. A manic depressive, one never knew, she could be up or she could be down. Heaven knows, she had enough to make her down. It was a strange relationship, platonic, not always harmonious, but she depended on him, and it was a commitment he had made to take care of her. What was she going to say to him writing a book, tapping away at a typewriter hour after hour. If he did this book – and he might be forced to, it might be the only way to get money for his work into the human aura – he would have to get a typewriter, ribbons, paper. A pawn shop, maybe. He liked pawn shops. He would often look in the windows, there were things you would never see anywhere else. Yes, a pawn shop would be a good place to find a typewriter, but it would all cost money and money was a commodity he did not possess. He had started a small business a couple of years ago. It was not doing badly when Ra'ab took it into her head that it was the wrong thing for them, and had withdrawn most of their savings, burned the bank notes, and he came home to find the chimney on fire. That was when they were living outside London. That was the end of that and the start of no money, or precious little.

Well, at least he could type although he only had the use of a finger and thumb on each hand, thanks to the Japanese and their tortures. They had captured him when he was flying medical mercy planes during the war with China, they had been sure he could give them information. His spine had been damaged too. That was another problem he would have to face, sitting for long periods of time. He would have to have the typewriter on his lap, they had no table and, besides, he could not manage to sit on a chair for long. He would sit on the floor, it was firmer than the squeaking bed. He would put his pillow behind his back. He could get the synopsis done within a matter of days. Already, though, he could feel warnings. Already he knew it could bring fame and adulation, notoriety and disbelief. He wanted neither. He wanted to be left alone to do his job. Before he made a decision he would have to consult with others in the astral.

It was a good walk back to Queensway and his back was painful, but he was used to pain. Hunger was worse. He had the pie in a paper bag, and the immediacy of his hunger spurred him on. If Ra'ab had not been at home, perhaps also hungry, he would have stopped somewhere to eat it, even in its frozen state. At least, they always saw that Ku'ei, their Siamese cat, had food. He loved the little creature, and had an understanding with her. As he turned the key and opened the door of the tall Victorian row house, he heard the landlady screaming at one of the other tenants about toilet paper again. She was obsessed with the idea that they were all stealing it, although what they were supposed to be doing with it was not ever clear.

He climbed the stairs, dark brown and dingy, managing to avoid her by stepping into the bathroom on the half-landing until she had disappeared, grumbling and cursing tenants under her breath. But there was no avoiding the smell of food, cabbage, boiled mutton, kippers, a conglomeration of cheap food that individually smelled awful but collectively repulsive. He kept his thoughts firmly focussed on the steak and kidney pie, the pastry crisp on the top, thick and soggy with delicious gravy on the bottom of the plate. For the moment he needed food. Tonight he would journey far, far away, out of the body, in an altered state altogether, and would get the answers and assurances he needed. For now he had to look after the dense physical body he inhabited, the vehicle he needed to do the work that had to be done.

Back in Regent Street, in the comfortable office high above the crowds, Charles and Cecil Banks remained silent for a few moments, neither knowing quite what to say and both conscious of the presence of the man who had just left.

"Well now, what d'you say to a drink? I have an excellent Scotch, you really should try it." Cecil recovered his composure first and got up to fetch glasses and whisky.

"Splendid, what a good idea!" Charles removed his spectacles and wiped them with a large silk handkerchief before replacing them. He took out his pocket watch and consulted it idly, without registering the time of day, or really knowing what he was doing. Shifting his position he said, "What, then, was your impression of this brilliant lama? I must admit to being highly impressed. There is something about him, to my mind, which alters the entire atmosphere."

"Hmm, yes, I would agree. A sort of magnetism, perhaps. Should one not be a little cautious? There is a feeling of dealing with the unknown." Cecil took a sip of his whisky and began to feel better. "I shall be extremely interested to see if he really can write."

"Cautious!" Charles expostulated. "Don't be ridiculous! The man is brilliant. I tell you, he'll write a book which will amaze us all – well not me, of course, because I discovered him in a sense. If you persist in being cautious of what you don't understand you'll never get anywhere, you'll never understand anything worth understanding. Anyway, the ball, as they say, is in his court now, and yours too. I've done my bit. If nothing comes of it, I shall be, let us truthfully say, extremely disappointed. We must just wait and see, and in the meantime – I have good progress to report to you on the second book, and I hope you have good reports for me on sales of the first."

And so they discussed business, touching base on all those matters important and not so important that have to do with books and publishing and earnings, and when it was time for him to go Charles shook hands and promised to deliver a completed manuscript within four months. As he reached the door he turned round, "Incidentally, Banks, you should get rid of that lift man. Gives a damned poor impression." He disappeared, mackintosh over his arm, fully intending to take the stairs to the ground floor.

* * *

It seems to me, so far as I can remember, that we did not see Dr. Ku'an after Mrs. Wood left until the day he arrived quite unexpectedly to show us the synopsis. It would be a matter of a month or so. Around that time there was a really heavy load of social obligations which left one feeling ragged and ungrounded simply by the nature of it, something like walking on quick sand all the time, so I was delighted when John, answering his knock on the door, brought him into the drawing room that evening after dinner. It was as a ray of sanity. "How lovely to see you," I cried, pulling up the hard-backed side chair he liked. "We've been wondering so much about your meeting with Charles, if it ever transpired."

"Thank you," he said, taking the chair. "I do hope I am not disturbing you, but I thought you might like to know how things went. The meeting certainly did transpire."

He was, as always, courteous and balanced. He was never effusive, never artificial in his manner. I remember noticing how gaunt and sallow he looked at that time. In the summer months his skin took on a beautiful golden warmth but in the winter he looked pale. Now he looked ill. He had been a tall man in his youth, six foot, he had told me, but now was perhaps three or four inches shorter because of the tortures he had endured. He was powerfully built, however, and still had immense strength in his arms. I expressed concern for his health, but he shrugged it off, wanting to focus on the purpose of his visit. He explained that Charles had been unable to offer him employment, but instead had taken him to see Cecil Banks. He explained his reluctance to write a book about his life, but that he had reached the conclusion that perhaps he had no choice. Both John and I were delighted. The possibility of him writing a book had never occurred to either of us. It would have the desired effect, so we both thought, (although for me it was not desired) of moving him out of the circle of our lives into the limelight where he would be surrounded by people of note in the literary world. I felt a pang of uncertainty.

Sensing or reading my thought he said, "I shall never forget you, for me you will always be present. I have had little assistance in my life, you know, so I value it highly. Now I am going to leave you, but before I go I have promised my wife that I would deliver a message to you, Mrs. Rouse. She would like to invite you to tea, and wonders if you would have time for that."

"Oh, but of course I would! How kind of her. Ask her to telephone me, won't you please, and we can arrange it."

I was pleased with the invitation, and, as much as anything else, anxious to meet this woman who was the wife of such a remarkable man.

From her voice on the telephone I knew she came from the north country. Being a northerner myself I am familiar with the various accents, so I placed her in my mind as a Cumbrian and, as it turned out, I was quite correct. Later, I learned that she was born and brought up on a farm in Cumberland. It seemed her father had been abusive, regarding her as lazy, and she had been very unhappy. She had left home early and gone in for nursing. All this I found out much later, as I say. This first day she had asked me to meet her in a restaurant, or tea shop, in Kensington High Street, and said I would recognize her because she would be wearing a certain thing, I do not recall exactly what it was, but let us say a green scarf. When I arrived at the appointed time the place was almost empty, three tables or so being occupied. I quickly looked around and spotted her immediately. She got up, and spoke with the voice I knew. She had already ordered tea and cakes, and as soon as I was seated opposite her began to pour the tea with no further ado.

She was talkative and friendly, clearly wishing to create a good impression, but actually making one feel slightly uncomfortable by the intensity of her manner. Despite that, I found her fascinating. She talked about such things as astrology, clairvoyance, telepathy in much the same way as I would have discussed a dance, the theatre or a point-to-point. These exotic subjects were commonplace to her. She had obviously studied, she had intellectualized, but because it was not truly a part of her, not knowledge and ability she had been born with, she found it necessary to talk about it. Her husband, on the other hand, seldom talked about exotic subjects in everyday life. When he did, it was so deeply a part of him that it seemed entirely natural, he might have been discussing the weather. Later, when he wrote about metaphysics, occult and esoteric subjects he found it boring and often said he hated writing. Despite that, he was always fully able, as any real teacher can, to simplify, explain, draw parallels. In metaphysical terms he was an Adept.

So was she, then, this wife of his, anything like I expected? No, perhaps not. In appearance she was plain, middle aged and rather overweight. Her hair was white, straight and unattractively cut, short, severe and unbecoming. She wore spectacles and no make-up. Later from the beautiful portrait photographs done by her first husband, Cyril Hoskins, which she kept on display, it was apparent that she had been striking in her youth, with excellent bone structure, a Nefertiti type profile and black hair, but this kind of beauty requires money and leisure to maintain, and she had been granted neither. She lived, one has to say, with the memory and this gave to her personality a narcissism which for the individual meeting her now was hard to understand. She had what I would call a strong character, her belief in herself was firm, even if others failed sometimes to see it as she did.

I wanted to know about the book, how the agent had liked the synopsis, if a publisher had been found. She was surprisingly noncommittal about it. Perhaps she was less than enthusiastic about a book and the prospect of fame for her husband. But I did learn that the agent had approved of the synopsis, and I supposed that when a publisher had been found, Dr. Ku'an would let us know, and indeed that was the case.

In retrospect, it seems strange that I was not curious as to how they met, but the truth is just that. I already had respect for Dr. Ku'an in a way I had never before respected anyone. He was on a different level from anyone else I was ever likely to meet, and so, although I would have been keenly interested in the minutest details concerning anyone else I might have come across and liked, in his case it never occurred to me to pry or question. I trusted him utterly. I was prepared to accept his wife on the same level, but of course she in no way equalled him. It would be unfair to expect her to, and as my story unfolds you will see why. The sad part, I think, is that it was hard for her not to occupy the limelight, the limelight he would have given anything to avoid.

* * *

Cecil Banks was of the old school. He had set ideas about certain things, and he saw no reason to change. He had always managed very well the way he was. Writers and publishers were his bread and butter, and he knew which side his bread was buttered on. They came in different types, often tricky to deal with, but he had them classified in his mind and knew pretty well which to put with which and how they would react. It was like horse racing. He knew where to place his bets. When Dr. Ku'an arrived in his office, however, only ten or fifteen days after their first meeting, and complete with what looked like a reasonably full synopsis by the size of it, he was taken by surprise. A synopsis was not something you just did in a matter of days like that, not if it was any good. Maybe it was not any good. Maybe Charles was barking up the wrong tree and he had been taken in. He wished the lama would sit down instead of standing there, waiting. It was unnerving.

"Ah, well now, Dr. Ku'an, so you decided to do the book after all? Splendid, splendid, really splendid news. Do sit down, won't you." Rubbing his hands together, he was at his most affable in an effort to dissemble his astonishment. The lama remained standing. "But – well – you realize of course that I may not have a chance to look at it for a week or two. Pressures, you know, pressures. Rest assured, though, I will deal with it and contact you. Now, do we have your telephone number?"

"I have no telephone. More to the point, I have no food on the table. I also have pressures." The lama's voice was low, but his words cut like steel. His eyes were hard. There was no doubt that he meant what he was saying. "I will return in one week, Mr. Banks. If you haven't had time or inclination to come to a decision in that time I will ask for my work to be returned to me. Good afternoon." He made his usual slight bow before turning towards the door and closing it quietly as he left.

Cecil was so startled he did not even ring for Miss Bartel to show the lama out. For a moment he sat there, then he reached for a cigar. What the devil! He had never had a client like this one. He was tempted to give the synopsis to Miss Bartel and tell her to hand it to the lama when he returned next week, and that would be the end of it, but his better self made him hesitate. The man looked ill, perhaps he was starving, it would look bad if he dropped dead. He took the pages out of the large manilla envelope and started to read. Half an hour later he rang for Miss Bartel. "I don't want to be disturbed for the next hour. If anyone wants me just tell them I am out for the rest of the day." An hour later he rang for her again. "Get me through to Mr. W - - -, will you, please?" And then, "Ah, Fred, how are you? Cecil Banks here. How are you placed for luncheon this week? The day after tomorrow? Yes, excellent. Berkeley Grill at one o'clock. I have something I think you'll like."

He mixed a drink and stared out of the window. It was only a synopsis but it got you, it moved you, it was like the lama himself, it took you to the unknown, it took you out of yourself. He hardly ventured to think what the book might be like. This kind of thing did not come along every day, in fact it was a rarity. It was compelling, it breathed life, it was genuine. He would take it home tonight, finish it, look at it again. But he hardly needed to, his experience told him all he wanted to know. Fred W— was one of the best in the publishing world, he only handled the best, his firm had a good reputation, had had for years, and he was no fool either. If he took it - and Cecil felt almost sure he would - well, they would have a winner.

And he did take it. By the time, a few weeks later, Dr. Ku'an returned to tell us the news, he had met the publisher and they had signed a contract. It had been agreed that they would pay him an advance on royalties.

"And what is the title?" I wanted to know, so excited I could barely contain my joy. Now they could eat better, they might move to a more comfortable place. I did not consider or realize the work he was having to undertake.

"The title will be 'The Third Eye.' I shall write under a different name, Tuesday Lobsang Rampa, T. Lobsang Rampa. In fact I'll probably change my name to Rampa legally. Easier that way, I think."

"So now we should call you Dr. Rampa, I suppose," John said, in a rather slighting voice.

"No, not at all. My friends call me Chen," he replied simply.

"Chen! What a lovely name and how well it suits you! We shall be honoured to call you by that name," I told him warmly, hoping to mitigate any insult he might have inferred from my husband. And the name did suit him.

He stayed only a short time that evening, and as he was leaving he turned and said, "The publisher wants me to bring him a chapter at a time within a certain time." With a wry smile he went on, "I'm a foreigner, after all, not always to be trusted, eh? Anyway, as I do the chapters, I'd like you to look them over, if that wouldn't be too much trouble."

"Oh, but we'd simply love to do that, wouldn't we John? We'd be delighted and honoured!" I told him.

John nodded his agreement. "Of course we'd be pleased, but Sheelagh has more time than I do, naturally. Anyway, this is excellent news, I'm sure you'll write a first class book." We were not directly responsible for the birth of this book, in reality Charles occupied that position, but it is an undisputed fact that without us it would not have happened.

CHAPTER THREE

My mother was a Victorian. Born near the end of Victoria's reign, admittedly, but still a Victorian. She lived to an advanced age, her life spanning almost the entire twentieth century. She was a remarkable woman and a difficult one, but she had some sound ideas, often unique to herself. She was sympathetic towards children and firmly held the belief that they should be surrounded by beautiful things from the earliest age, the premise being that it would foster a sense and appreciation of beauty. If things were broken, finger-marked and generally messed up, no matter, it was all in a good cause.

When I was small I loved to paint and draw, and to help the creative impulse along, and in keeping with my mother's philosophy, I was given a rather lovely antique walnut davenport. It should really be Davenport, capital 'D,' I think, because these particular little desks, or, more correctly, chest-of-drawers with a sloping desk top, were named after a Captain Davenport who, so I believe, had the first one made by the cabinet makers known as Gillow, to be installed in his cabin when he took to the high seas.

I loved my Davenport and spent hours perched on a chair made especially for me, with longer legs than usual, giving life to my childish imagination with pencil and brush. I cannot help thinking of this as I sit in front of a rather nasty plastic computer, a wonder of the modern world, but soulless. Could it be that if I were sitting at my beautiful little walnut Davenport with pen in hand, I would see in my mind's eye the picture taking shape more clearly? Could it be that I would write with greater fluency and skill? It is more than possible. Could my mental picture be clearer, could it be even more magical? But there is no point in wondering; the computer is here to stay.

With my imaginary brush I wet the imaginary paper, and as I do so I travel back down the years through the storehouse of memories and attempt to put the events of my story in order, to make a coherent whole, and paint it as it happened so long ago.

It was during the writing of 'The Third Eye' that I came to know the Rampa's well. Looking back it seems amazing that Chen was able to write a book of any sort in the cramped, noisy, disruptive conditions in which he and Ra'ab lived, but then he was no ordinary man. He not only produced a book, he produced a classic of charm and beauty that lifted one from the mundane, was inspirational and comforting as well as being a delight to read. He put himself into that book so simply. It was an account of his early life, and it had depth and knowledge, it contained mystical, esoteric parts, and it was amusing and light in other parts. Tibet had been invaded by the British in 1904, and then by the Chinese in 1910, but by 1911 the invaders had been driven out – for the time being at least – and 'The Third Eye' was set in a time of peace when the 13th Dalai Lama, the one whom many regard as the last true Incarnation, was in control of the country.

With two fingers and two thumbs, an old typewriter, a pillow at his back and sitting on the floor, Chen produced a small masterpiece, a book that would be translated into many different languages and sell worldwide, a book whose author would face criticism and scorn as well as adulation, but a book that would survive. Moreover, it still sells fifty years, or more, after its conception.

Even the writing of it was not all plain sailing yet he navigated the turbulence with dexterity. One also has to wonder about Ra'ab's part in this, how could she tolerate the ghastly tap, tap, tapping, of a typewriter (and they were noisy things) day in and day out without going completely mad? How could she bear the neighbours rapping on the wall from next door, and the neighbours from below banging on their ceiling with a broom handle when they could take no more? But somehow she did, and she deserves credit.

True to his word, he brought a chapter at a time for us to read. I am honestly not quite sure if it was a token of appreciation, or because he wanted to see the effect of his writing on the uninitiated. He was heard to remark quite often that his biggest problem was in knowing what it was that others did not know. He realized that things which were commonplace to him were often completely beyond the range of comprehension to most others, and with John and me he had a reasonable sounding board. I am reminded of the first day he arrived at our house with the opening chapter of 'The Third Eye' in his hand.

We lived in a quiet street just north of Kensington Gardens. A little further up the street stood an imposing synagogue which I assumed to be the Jewish equivalent of St. Margaret's, Westminster, the Anglican place of worship where smart society weddings, christenings, and any other corner-stone event of life took place on an impressive level for the sophisticated and wealthy. The synagogue was on the opposite side of the street from us, and the children loved to stand on the garden wall and watch the goings on through the black iron railings placed on top of the wall, with a running commentary from Jarvis causing acute embarrassment to Fenella.

On this particular day we had just returned from a walk in the park, that is, Jarvis, Chester and myself. Fenella was at school. It was a chilly, brisk sort of day. Jarvis had been sailing his boat in the Round Pond and had dashed in after it, soaking his boots and woollen leggings, and even the bottom of his coat. I was annoyed with him, and annoyed with myself for letting it happen, and quickly bundled him into the push-chair I always took with us for just such an emergency, for the numerous times he fell off or into something, or for when he was just too tired to walk home. I strapped him in firmly and set off for home, irritated that Chester seemed unable to keep up when I was in a hurry to get home and change Jarvis into dry clothes before he caught cold. As we neared the house I could see an event was taking place at the synagogue, large black cars were everywhere, exquisitely dressed women and men with top hats were alighting and crossing the street. They were in my way, and I needed to get home before my small son caught cold. I was impatient and annoyed.

"Mama, Mama, look, look, it's a wedding, a wedding," Jarvis strained at the belt keeping him in his push-chair, he wanted to get out and join in with what he saw, correctly, as a wedding. Black clothes for funerals, bright colours for weddings and christenings, that was what I had told them, and at least he had taken it in, although his habit of repeating everything twice was utterly maddening when one was already irritated.

"Yes, darling, you're absolutely right, it must be a wedding," I agreed, "but let's get home and and take off those wet things first, then you can stand on the wall and watch." I gave a tug at Chester's leash to make him hurry. He rewarded me with an extra and unnecessary lifting of his hind leg, making me feel mean and guilty. He really could not care less who was getting married or buried, he just wanted justice and a bit of consideration from this human to whom he was so loyal.

So there was Jarvis, dry and wearing clean, warm shoes and socks, standing on the wall and supervising the elaborate nuptials of an eminent and wealthy member of the Jewish community, his commentary worthy of Richard Dimbleby, when who should come through the gate but Chen, with a large manilla envelope in his hand. Jarvis jumped off the wall, and ran to my side. I knew he had reservations about Chen, but I was unclear as to what and why.

"How wonderful to see you!" I greeted Chen. "Can it be that you are bringing the first chapter?"

"How did you guess? Yes, here it is. This is my copy, the publisher has his, and now we have to wait and see what he thinks." Turning to Jarvis he said, "Good day, Jarvis." The child did not answer, but clung to my skirt, burying his face in the fabric for all the world as though he were an ostrich in the sand.

"Jarvis, it's poor manners not to reply when someone speaks to you," I rebuked him. He looked at me defiantly, and without a word let go of my skirt and ran through the partly opened gate, off down the street, dodging the unusual number of people on their way to the synagogue. He had not gone more than a few yards when he fell down, and I knew he had succumbed to an attack of asthma, my dreaded fear always that one day he would not survive, one day he would fall down and not get up. I started to go after him, but Chen put his hand on my arm. "No," he said, "let me go."

I stood outside the gate watching as Chen made his slow and deliberate way to the small boy lying on the pavement. Why was he not running, I wondered, why did the people not stop to help? But they chose to ignore something unpleasant, they were on their way to an event, they were dressed in clothes unsuitable for dealing with illness. I might have reacted in exactly the same manner in their place. What could they do, anyway? All the same, at that moment I could have killed them – cheerfully!

As he came level with Jarvis, Chen stood for a moment and regarded him lying on the ground in a heap, fighting for breath. Then he knelt down beside him and touched his head, speaking to him. What an unlikely scene! The small boy on the ground, the man dressed in black kneeling beside him, the passersby, decked out in their finery and intent on their function, in their own space. It was like two separate worlds interlocked but not touching. Then, as if by a miracle, Jarvis stopped gasping, his body became still, and slowly he rose to his feet and walked back towards me, his head down. "Mama, I'm sorry." He took hold of Chester's collar, and led him inside the house. What on earth could have happened in those brief few minutes to cause such a change in him.? I looked to Chen for a clue, but received nothing. Casually referring to his book, he remarked, "I don't expect it will take you more than a day or two to read it. Would it be agreeable to you if I call in three days to see you, and get your reaction?"

"Yes, yes, of course. We'll read it tonight after the children are in bed. But, Chen, what happened, whatever happened with Jarvis?"

"Jarvis? Do you really want me to tell you?" He paused, and then went on, "You overindulge him. He knows it, and he knows that I know it, that's why he doesn't want to have anything to do with me. Small children are often more aware of reality than adults. As they grow older they get the ability stamped out of them by what is called reason, it's a pity really, but there is it."

"I overindulge him? I don't follow. What has that to do with his asthma?" I was hurt but also genuinely puzzled.

"Well, its a psychological reaction, a sort of unconscious emotional blackmail. He won't have another attack."

"But what did you do? Do you mean he's cured? I don't understand."

"Don't try to understand, don't try to reason it all out. Just accept it and one day you will understand. But as you are so curious I will tell you one thing for your own good; Jarvis is overindulged, as I said, but you indulge him to indulge yourself. If you really want to help that child you will loosen the ties that bind him to you. Think about it, I know what I'm talking about." He went towards the gate, then turned back. "Don't feel embarrassed to correct any mistakes in my grammar or spelling, will you." And off he went, pulling the tall wooden gate shut behind him.

* * *

That night John was out doing whatever it was he did that I was not privy to. I had ceased to think about it. The trouble was, though, that it was there between us and limited our conversation more or less to the weather. English weather, fortunately, is changeable and can be quite an extensive and inexhaustible topic. After the children were in bed I took a tray – scrambled eggs, fruit and a glass of wine – to the drawing room where there was a good fire burning. The heavy gold curtains were drawn. I felt relaxed and comfortable. As I ate my supper my mind ran over the day. It had been such a strange affair with Jarvis, the way he recovered, the way he said he was sorry. Sorry! He never said he was sorry except under pressure when he had been really naughty. I was reluctant to believe that he was cured, that some miracle cure had taken place. His illness has become such a bete noire with me, so ingrained that, although I dreaded it, I was unable to let it go. As for indulging Jarvis to please myself - well, that was ridiculous, complete and utter nonsense.

I sipped the wine, a good one, satisfying, robust, and my eyes wandered to the pastel drawing of Fenella which hung over the mantelpiece. We had had it done a couple of years earlier, and I had never been too sure about it. There was something there that made me uneasy, although no one else seemed to notice it. Now as I looked at the little girl over the rim of my glass I knew suddenly what it was that troubled me. The child who stared back was unhappy, sulky, dissatisfied. True, she had not enjoyed the sittings, but the artist had gone beyond that, she had portrayed the inner feelings of this child who was my daughter, and she had portrayed those inner feelings very clearly. Perhaps it was this realization, this revelation, that caused it, no matter what it was, something caused a tiny crack in the hard, tough shell of denial with which I habitually surrounded myself, caused a chink of light to penetrate. I thought of George, a clever doctor, a friend whom I admired, I thought of him telling me that Jarvis' asthma was a mother/son thing, and how I had secretly laughed at him for saying so. I thought of Chen, someone else I admired and trusted, who was really saying the same thing, but in a more direct, explicit way. Could they be trying to tell me something about the way I brought up my children? Abruptly I shut out the thought. I was getting paranoid, neurotic, it must be the wine, yes, that's what it was, wine making me maudlin and morbid. I had to stop even considering such nonsense.

Chen's envelope lay on my drum table. I got up, crossed the room and opened the flap carefully. I could see at a glance that the pages were carefully typed, well spaced, easy to read. I had had no previous idea of what the book would be like, Chen had not discussed it with either of us. If I had thought about it at all it was that it would be a little beyond me, serious, perhaps full of dissertations on religion and philosophy, so I was completely unprepared for the opening paragraph:

' 'Oe. Oe. Four years old and can't stay on a horse! You'll never make a man! What will your noble father say?' With this old Tzu gave the pony – and luckless rider – a hearty thwack across the hindquarters and spat in the dust.'

Four years old! A little boy like Jarvis! I stood there reading, I had to read on, I was immediately there in Tibet, I could see a little boy, a horse, a fierce old groom spitting in the dust, the golden domes of the Potala gleaming in the distance. I was lost in it, my troubles forgotten, I was there with that small boy. As I look back it astounds me to think that I was the first person, apart I suppose from Ra'ab, to read words that would cross the world and give hope to millions. Words that were to cause controversy sparked by jealousy which in the longrun was nothing compared to the message they carried. Words that survived.

I took the pages over to my chair beside the fire, and settled myself down to read them. Often it is hard to get into a book, but with this there was no such difficulty. The reader was immediately engaged and compelled to read on. It was skillful in its simplicity, clarity and gentle introduction to life in a far away land without being in any way exotic. I could see Chen as a mischievous small boy, strictly brought up, toughened up, his father one of the leaders of the country. I could picture him flying kites, carving, doing archery, long jumping, stilt-walking, playing with the cats, as well as studying lessons. I could see his mother, an autocrat who ran matters as she liked them to be run in her household. The chapter dealt with the fact that at the age of seven Chen's future would be revealed by astrologers, and a large party would be held at his home for this event. One sensed the dread of the small boy, faced by an unknown future, by the party being held, by the knowledge that he would be sent on his way by a stern father with no chance of returning home. But this was what he had been toughened up for, this was real life, and he had no options.

When I had finished reading I laid the pages aside. I was immensely enthused, and if they had had a telephone I would have rung up then and there to tell Chen how much I liked it. As it was, I had to wait until a few days later when I saw him and was able to tell him face to face how much I enjoyed his writing, and the whole feeling of this first chapter.

This was the start of weeks of reading the book chapter by chapter, weeks which ran into months, because there were delays along the way. For me, it was ideal. It enabled me to digest what I was reading in a way impossible if the book had been completed and then handed to me to read, in which case I would have taken it at a gallop, and it was because of this that I came to know the Rampa's so well. I am sure they would never have invited me to the dreary rooming house they lived in if it were not for the discussions we had about the book, but as it turned out, I went there regularly.

They had moved from the house in Queensway, the place Mrs. Wood had supposedly taken care of, but they were still close by and in a similar situation. One rooming house is not much different from the next. Moving was a way of life to them and I had already formed the opinion that they were somewhat nomadic, both of them having a horror of putting down roots and becoming in any way bound or attached to earthly things. It may as well have been that the new place was not quite so confining for writing, perhaps the walls were thicker, the house better constructed so that noise such as typing did not carry so easily. I am only surmising, but it is really of no consequence. It was a place to live, no more. They were restless and always would be. There was a necessity for them to experience, and then move on.

The room they occupied was on the first floor, what would have been the drawing room floor, of a large early Victorian row house which had seen better days, and they probably had one of the best rooms in the place. The house originally might have been owned by a merchant or some kind of businessman. Middle class people had money then, they had large families, they lived well. There might have been five, six or more children, some might not have survived childhood. There would have been a cook, a butler, perhaps a footman, a parlour maid, one or two housemaids. There would have been a nanny and a nursery maid. At the back of the house in the mews, they would have kept horses for the carriage, and a coachman to look after the horses. A family in those days was an entity, and to a psychic, such as Chen, there must have been a host of impressions lingering around the fabric of the place. My feeling is that he was expert at 'shutting out,' otherwise life would have been intolerable.

Their accommodation was just a small part of what once had been a large, and probably lovely room and it was left with the saving grace of possessing a charming long window. The room had a gas fire with a meter into which one put coins, a small gas cooker, two beds separated by a screen, and basic furniture such as a chest-of-drawers, two chairs and an easy chair which was usually occupied by Ku'ei, the seal point Siamese cat, sleeping on her blanket, or appearing to sleep yet in reality missing nothing. The myna bird had not survived, it had been rescued by Chen from a bad situation but was already struggling when it came to them. Even the spiders from our garage were not enough to revive the poor little creature. So when I first visited them Ku'ei was their only pet.

They had no wish for possessions then or ever, but what bothered them was the lack of privacy, the noise, the conflicting auric vibrations from others so close at hand, and the constant interference of the landlady. I forget the street number, but I do remember the location very clearly, only a few streets from our own house, yet it might have been a different world. There was litter on the street, the people who inhabited the neighbourhood were part of an homogenous mass surviving on, or very slightly above, the poverty level. They lived day to day with the knowledge that they had to hang onto life although they had long since ceased to wonder why simply because there seemed to be no answer. There were no smart little window boxes here overflowing with flowers, no wrought iron railings, no trim balconies with trailing ivy geraniums. It was far from being a slum, yet there was an air of desperation, a hopelessness which in the end destroys. In a strange way it suited Chen, or perhaps it would be more accurate to say it suited his study of the human condition. He was recording it as it was, recording it from the inside, not as some intellectual researcher looking on and making erudite commentaries, but as one of the denizens of the place, suffering the same poverty and degradation.

I remember well the first time I visited. Ra'ab had rung me up and suggested I might like to take tea with them. It was really in order to talk about something in the book which I had not fully understood, and wanted to ask about. She used to make telephone calls from a call box on the corner of the street where they lived, and in our hurry to finish the conversation before the coins ran out, we arranged a day and time, but I quite forgot to ask the number of their room at the address she had given me. Oh well, I thought, it will not be a problem, there will surely be someone there I can ask.

When the day arrived Chester was unwell. He was getting on in years and I worried about him. Fenella was at school, but Jarvis promised me in a very grown-up manner that he would take care of Chester while I was out. I knew he liked the feeling of responsibility, and I knew that Mrs. Wood's successor was a reliable woman who would supervise both Jarvis and Chester. Nevertheless, I was anxious and preoccupied, unable to put off the visit as there was no way of getting in touch with the Rampa's, so I dressed to go out without really considering how I should dress, it was just a question of getting ready, getting the visit over and returning home.

I decided to walk as it was a pleasant day and would probably only take fifteen minutes or so. I was used to shopping in Moscow Road, but had never penetrated further north, since our usual walks were in Kensington Gardens or Hyde Park, and I was in for a surprise. Turning a corner just a couple of streets beyond my customary shopping ground I entered new territory, and the change was astonishing. It was rundown and dirty looking, the people had a hangdog, down-at-heel look, or rather, that was the impression because, in fact, there were not many people around. A man lounging on a doorstep called out as I passed by: 'Get back on yer' beat luv, yer ain't gonna to get no takers 'ere.' He cackled in a lewd and insolent manner. What could he be talking about, was it not policemen who had beats? Whatever it was, it was nothing complimentary, that was clear, and my feeling of compassion was turning to anger. But I ignored him and continued on my way, counting the houses as I went. Then from down the street there came the sudden blare of a radio, giving me a jolt, and shrieks of laughter. It was gruesome and I was beginning to wish I had never agreed to come, I was beginning to feel conspicuous in high heels, a smart little hat, handbag and gloves. This was a poor district and I was aware of being stared at. What pathetic dregs they were, the people seemed like the remnants of humanity and the place smelled of decay. What on earth was I doing here? Was I in the right street? Could this really be where the Rampa's lived?

Eventually, I arrived at the number I had been searching for, and mounted the broad steps to the front door. There were coloured glass panes in the upper part of the door, and on the wall to the side was an array of numbered push bells, no names beside them, presumably because the tenants were constantly on the move. I pushed the first bell and as if by magic a door in the basement area was thrust open by a sour-faced woman with a mop in her hand, who emerged and stood looking up at me. She remained there surveying me for a moment dispassionately, then removed the cigarette dangling from her lips.

"Well, wot yer want 'ere, ducks? Lookin' for somethink, are yer?" Her voice was hostile, defensive. "We're decent folk 'ere, we are." Her frizzy hair was dyed an unlikely auburn hue, and from my vantage point above her on the steps I could see the grey roots. She wore carpet slippers with holes in the toes.

"Oh, I'm sorry to disturb you. I must have pushed the wrong bell. I'm looking for the Rampa's."

“Them wot’s changed their name, eh? Push number seven.” And she disappeared as fast as she had come, slamming the door behind her.

In answer to my pushing number seven Ra’ab soon appeared at the door, and asked me to follow her up the stairs. The walls were painted dark brown, the stairs were painted brown, the threadbare carpet was brown, the only relief being where the paint had worn off, showing traces of white undercoat. There was a musty smell, as though no fresh air ever penetrated, and as we ascended the stairs I could smell cooking, strong fish cooking, maybe mackerel or something equally unpleasant. Then the stairs turned, and in a minute we were on the first floor. Ra’ab opened one of the three doors facing us, and we entered their room. Instantly the atmosphere changed. There was a faint haze caused by a stick of Indian incense placed in a brass container on a small table beside the bed Chen lay upon, the smoke spiraling and gently swirling, filling the room with its fragrance. As nearly as I was able to identify it, the smell was of musk roses. Incense is used to raise one’s vibrations, and this was exactly what it achieved. The stick was long and thick, quite unlike the puny, short sticks found in gift shops, for instance, this was of the kind used in serious meditation or praying, the kind used in esoteric work where higher senses are called into play. The powerful, rich, deep fragrance has a strong effect on the senses, uplifting and refining. It was as though one had come from a gloomy pit of poverty into a restful, pleasant place. At that time the Rampa’s could barely afford the luxury of incense, but that one stick had been lit for my coming, and immediately I felt at ease, almost as if I had come home, or come to some place where I belonged.

The proportions of the room were dreadful, the walls dingy and the furnishings meagre. The gas fire and gas cooker were ugly, but none of it mattered. By upbringing and inclination I was – and still am – extremely sensitive and critical of environment and living space, however, for the first time in my life I felt an inkling that my values could possibly be wrong, perhaps I placed too much value on the wrong things. Which is not to say that I was instantly converted, far from it, I fear.

Whenever I had seen Chen previously, he had been dressed in a black suit with a black bow tie and usually wore a pink shirt, but as he rested at home on his bed he had exchanged his jacket for a dressing gown, and he had the little Siamese cat curled up on his lap. His hands were clasped on his chest, which was typical and customary and the way he invariable rested when at home and not occupied with work or hobbies. He exuded tremendous strength and a rare inner peace. It was like entering a place of harmony, but not hallowed; it was too genuine to be in any way holy or religious, it was just comfortable and safe. Ra'ab had the kettle boiling and made tea. We sat and drank it, and talked about the book. By this time we were on Chapter Four, and I was perplexed at the harshness of the lamasery. I wanted him to explain to me why it was so harsh, what about the religious side of it, what about the Buddhist gentle approach to life that Westerners believed existed in the East? He answered me satisfactorily, but I could see that he felt the impossibility, or the near impossibility, of writing about his life for people so divergent from him in thought and belief. He was wondering if he could actually get through the cultural barrier. He did, I would say, get through it very effectively, and for that skill he was criticized later by those who saw themselves as scholars, and found his writing too popular, desecrating, they felt, something sacred not to be shared by outsiders.

I explained that Chester was unwell and that I was uneasy leaving him for too long. They understood, and as I rose to leave Chen said, "I hope you'll come again soon. Just now there's a slight hitch with the publisher, someone somewhere in the nether regions of the firm is asking for more proof of who I am." He shrugged as though it were of no importance, but I knew by the very fact of downplaying it that he was hurt. "It seems that some other firm recently published a book purporting to be autobiographical," he went on, "and it turned out to be a fabrication. There was trouble. Mr. W-- doesn't want trouble with me, or rather with my book, but how can I give proof other than what I've already given? They've seen my papers from Chungking, my medical certificates. You know how it is, though, once a doubt has been put in someone's mind, it can be fed, it grows. It's a negative and negative forces are much, much stronger than positive forces on this earth."

I stood and looked at him, ponderingly. "Isn't it proof enough that you know so well the habits and customs of your country, the places and events? No one could have fabricated that. Why, you know the names of roads, and things, in Lhasa far better than I know names in London. It would be impossible to fabricate the things you write about. Anyone who doubts what you have written and needs proof of who you are, whatever that may mean, must be a complete idiot!! You are who you are."

"Well, well - yes, but there it is. They are getting in so-called experts to confirm things I have written. Of course, it will be all right in the end, but no one likes to be thought of as a liar. The funny thing is, though, that I am doubtful of these experts! I don't suppose any of them has lived in Tibet for any length of time, and certainly not in a lamasery."

"Well, we have to let Sheelagh go," Ra'ab chimed in. "It just means that the book might not be done as quickly, and it's annoying as they only pay when Chen produces a chapter." She was essentially practical.

By the time I got home Jarvis was deeply engaged in some building process in the garden, one of those that require water and stones for dams and result in wet feet. He greeted me casually, he was otherwise occupied.

Chester was lying behind the front door on his mat waiting for me, and I knelt down beside him, putting my arms around his neck. He snuffled and waggled his round, brown body, telling me he loved me. It was impossible to visualize life without him, but it was inevitable, not immediate, but it would happen, and the time was getting nearer. Who was going to listen to my woes when Chester was not around to lend an ear? John, frankly, was one dimensional when it came to understanding anything beyond the mundane. Cordelia, well yes, but not quite like Chester, she refused to put up with anything that she considered weak or complaining. Chester, on the other hand, put up with everything. I kissed his ears and told him that I loved him, too. It made me remember a dream I had had a few nights previously.

Chester was there in the dream smoking a cigar. Dogs do not talk, we all know that, nor do they usually smoke cigars, but, all the same, he was telling me I had to decide. He was telling me quite firmly that my tightrope act was over and I had to make a choice. Then I realized I was in an aeroplane flying high above the earth, one of those small aircraft where you can see all around as you sit in the cockpit. I could see the curve of the earth. I saw the black, cruel sea far below ready to swallow me up if I did not decide, if I dallied any longer I would be pushed over into that terrible, final ocean. I looked up, and there was my mother flying on a broomstick, calling to me. She was wearing her sable coat, which struck me as odd on a broomstick, and a tall hat straight from the early 16th century when witchcraft was at its zenith. Was I to jump into the sea, or follow the broomstick? The devil or the deep blue sea. And then in the far, far distance there was a light twinkling. I had the sensation that it was going to save me. It drew closer closer and became brighter and brighter and more and more constant, and then – – I woke up! It was a vivid dream, so real that I remembered it in every detail. Chester did resemble Winston Churchill, and Churchill did, indeed, speak. My mother did read "The Lancashire Witches" by Harrison Ainsworth to us, my brother and myself, as a bedtime story when we were barely out of the cradle. She was fascinated by witchcraft and witches, so it was logical to see her as a witch flying on a broomstick. I have already said, you know, that she had some unique ideas, but as for the soundness of that one – the choice of our bedtime stories – it could be up for discussion!

* * *

Every story has a cast of characters who make it what it is. One of my favourite characters is long since gone, she was old then. Margaret Martin was her name. To most of her mistresses, those who employed her, she was known as 'Martin.' To me she was 'Martie,' but then, I was not truly her mistress, although she treated me with the greatest respect because she was that kind of person.

Martie had been a lady's maid in her heyday. Sometimes she told me and the children about the houses she had worked in, about her ladies, about their families, about what went on below stairs. She was a wonderful historian, accurate, colourful and amusing. At the end of the day I hated to see her put on her hat and go on her way. It was not just the pile of mended and darned clothes she left in her wake, the let down hems and let out seams, the hats with pretty new trimmings, it was that she added a special intangible something to our lives. Her gentle grace was almost a thing of the past – even then.

Martie's ladies were from another era, and they were enchanting. For the most part, they had lived in immensely grand houses, and were themselves immensely grand ladies. Martie had seen life on a lavish scale, she had travelled wherever her current lady was bound for, she was there at smart house parties, brilliant balls, palaces, embassies. To these ladies the world was their oyster and Martie was a necessary component. Without her loving hand, they could never have appeared dressed and coifed, poised and elegant. She had learned discretion and tact, wisdom and duty. She was sublimely satisfied with life because she adhered to her creed that to give is to receive, and it worked for her one hundred percent.

Martie came to our house every other week. She arrived punctually at nine o'clock, a diminutive figure dressed in black, with a felt hat in winter and a panama hat in summer. Her skirts were long, but one could glimpse high button boots encasing neat little feet. She always clasped in her gloved hand a carpet bag which contained her sewing things and her lunch. Her bright eyes shone out from a lined and wrinkled face, overflowing with personality.

Every other Tuesday morning at nine o'clock, when we heard her gentle rap, rap, rap, as she reached up for the frog's leg and gently tapped it on the brass plate, the children would dash to the door, Chester following not far behind to join in the fun. "Mama, Mama, it's Martie, it's Martie. Come quick, come quick," Jarvis urged me on. She would be standing there smiling, gently stroking their fair heads, never one to spoil or excite children, but almost one of them by her tiny stature, and sweet, uncomplicated outlook on life. She would come upstairs to my bedroom, remove her hat pins carefully, then lay her hat on the dressing table. She had an astonishing variety and number of hats, relics of her days in service, beautiful, expensive hats finished with by her ladies, and passed on to her. She was constantly re-trimming with an ingenious array of feathers, flowers, ribbons, and fruits. They were almost works of art, those hats.

Before she did anything else she would go to the bathroom. She was aged and much too refined to ever joke about body parts breaking down as one gets older, we just knew they did, and that the bathroom was a necessity. Then she would sit down at the foot of the bed and begin her work. Fenella would sit on the floor cross-legged, and Jarvis would hug the mahogany bedpost and gaze at her, and then jump up on the bed to listen to her stories.

She was a little wary of Chester. She was only accustomed to sporting or lap dogs, and would tell of the small spaniels she had met at Blenheim Palace, brown and white they were, playful, affectionate little creatures, pretty too. Some of them would go out with the gentlemen shooting, to flush out game, and others, of a more loving temperament, or too elderly for hunting, would stay at home with the ladies. I made up my mind to own one of those spaniels some day.

When the longcase clock standing on the landing outside my bedroom chimed noon with its slow, deep voice, Martie would take her sandwich, piece of cake, cup with loose tea leaves already in it, out of the carpet bag, and would make her way downstairs to the kitchen, where she would fill the kettle with water and place it on the Aga to boil. If I had so much as offered to make the tea and bring it upstairs she would have been confused and offended. It would not have been proper, and would have thrown her out completely. After lunch the children went for a siesta, and I often lay down on my bed while she continued to sew and talk to me.

Since my first visit to the Rampa's, two or three weeks had elapsed during which time I had revisited twice more, taking care to dress in old, plain clothes. Chapter Five was completed, and I noticed that Chen had dealt with the question of severity in the lamaseries, so I felt useful in a sense; other readers, no doubt, would have asked the same question, and now he had answered it. The next day, after my third visit, it was Martie's day to come, and when she had eaten lunch and Jarvis had gone for his nap I lay down on the bed. Without looking up, she said, "Are you feeling well, madam? I have noticed you seem poorly lately."

I was taken aback. I had no idea that I seemed unwell, although it was a fact that I felt at odds with myself and the world. But then, Martie was an observant, wise person, interested in the welfare of others. "Well, yes, Martie, it's true, I don't feel as I should. For one thing I'm expecting another baby, but that shouldn't make me feel the way I do. I should be happy about that instead of - oh, I don't know - I just feel terribly unsettled, unfocussed, unable to cope with anything. I feel as if I'm stretched to the limit, somehow. I'm frightened at how I feel because I can't explain it. You know about my headaches and hay fever, but it seems to be getting worse all the time."

Talking about it was not a good idea, I decided. It made me feel weepy and even more stupid and inept. There was no room for such feelings in the circle we moved in, no understanding or sympathy, only mockery. It showed you were not able to toe the line, you were a failure. I turned away from Martie before she could see the tears in my eyes.

She continued with her sewing, the needle went in and out, in and out, she drew the thread, the needle went in and out, in and out. I turned my head back to her and looked at her hands as she sewed, the fingers so gnarled but so nimble, the flesh so white and soft, only the barest sprinkling of little brown age spots. Then she said, "When I was in India with Lady Rendl her young daughter became ill. She wouldn't speak to people, she wouldn't go out, she was very sad. His Lordship had no patience with it, he said to m'lady, 'Louise (that was their daughter's name, Louise) Louise is mad, she's just like your aunt, mad, it runs in your family. She'll end up being locked up in an asylum just like your aunt.'

"But m'lady wouldn't hear of it. She came from an ancient family, real aristocrats they were, whereas he was, if you'll excuse my saying so madam, jumped up, not the same at all. Her lineage was of the best, Scottish with a touch of French way, way back. It was unfair of him to say her aunt was mad. For sure, she was confined in one of those places where they put mad people, but she had had an accident out hunting. One day she was out with the Quorn and something happened, no one really knew what, but they got her up out of a ditch and she was broken all over. Poor lady, she was never the same again. But madness didn't run in Her Ladyship's family like he said it did. She was a saint, m'lady was, never said a word about how difficult m'lord was with her. Oh, madam, if you could have seen her when I had her dressed for a ball - - you never saw any lady so beautiful, so proud and regal." Martie stopped sewing and gazed out of the window, overcome by the poignancy of her memories

Of course, we had heard about Lady Rendl before because she was one of Martie's favourite ladies , but I was beginning to wonder what this was leading up to, what it had to do with my feeling unwell, when Martie, with a big sigh continued her story. "M'lady never went to doctors, she had no time for them. 'One day they say this, Martin, and the next day they say that,' she'd tell me. If she felt poorly with a cold or a headache she'd go to her cupboard where she had a whole lot of little bottles with tiny pellets in them, and she'd put a few under her tongue, 'homopathy', I think it was called, something like that. You see, madam, she knew about different things, m'lady did, always open to different things. A real aristocrat, she was. But she worried about Lady Louise, poor thing, oh, how she worried! Nothing seemed to help that young woman, nothing at all. Well, it seems that some lady who came for dinner one evening told her about this Indian gentleman who could see what was wrong with people and cure them. So Her Ladyship sent for him. She didn't tell m'lord because he would just have laughed – 'What! A native!' he'd have said. 'Witchcraft,' that's what he'd have said. He didn't have her breeding, you see, madam. He wasn't the same at all as she was.

"So this Indian gentleman came, and he took Lady Louise away with him up to the hills for several months. When she came back she was cured and happy. The Indian gentleman had made her better. She never did marry, although I'm sure a lot of young gentlemen would have liked to marry her. Instead, she started a colony for lepers and worked there herself for years. She did a lot of good work, and all because that Indian gentleman knew what was wrong with her. M'lady said he called it a sickness of the soul."

"Well, Martie, that's really interesting. So do you think I have a sickness of the soul?" I was half teasing her, but she took it seriously.

"Madam, I really couldn't say, but I do think you should talk to the foreign gentleman who comes here. I do think he would know. I think he is the same kind as the Indian gentleman who cured Lady Louise."

Instead of dismissing her idea I turned it over in my mind. Martie was one of those unaffected people who still, even as adults and aged citizens, have the clarity of vision of children. As Chen himself had explained it to me when talking about Jarvis, that thing called reason had not completely taken them over, they still were in touch with inherent knowledge, still (as I later came to understand it) in close touch with their Overself. So I took heed of her. Talk to Chen ? I could do that, but not while he was writing the book, he had far too much to preoccupy him without my worries.

But Martie was not one to let things slide. John was in the habit of running her home to her tiny flat in Pimlico Road at the end of the day, and that evening as she was leaving the house and John was waiting for her in the car she took my hand in hers. "Now, madam, remember what I said. When I come next time I hope to hear that you have talked to the foreign gentleman."

Without really knowing what I was saying I replied, "Yes, Martie, I will, I promise I will."

"Good, that's good. You know, madam, you must first look after your health," were her parting words, as she walked carefully down the path to the gate.

As I watched her, it seemed to me that she was a lot older than she said she was, it seemed to me that she was terribly frail. When she arrives in heaven, I thought, whatever her particular heaven may be, she will be hailed and greeted and applauded, they might even have champagne for her, in fact, they will certainly have champagne for her! I had made her a promise and I had to keep it, how could one not?

* * *

We had decided to send Jarvis to a sort of preschool. It was a small group of children, and was run by a pleasant woman who had little children of her own, the forerunner of today's daycare, I would say. He just went for three or four hours a day, and actually enjoyed it. A couple of days after Martie's visit I was on my way home after dropping both children at their respective schools when I saw Chen walking along the street, obviously on his way to our house.

"Oh, I'm so glad to see you," he greeted me as I pulled up beside him. "Are you all right?"

"Won't you get in? Come home and have a cup of tea with me." I opened the car door and he climbed in beside me. "Of course, I'm all right," I answered his question as I put the car in gear and we set off. "Why wouldn't I be?"

"Only that you've been truly bugging me!" It was hard to tell if he was serious or not. He had a habit of saying outlandish things with a straight face, often things that had more than a grain of truth in them, and you could take it or leave it. "Bugging you? What on earth do you mean?"

"Telepathy. It's not like a telephone where you can turn off the ringer. If someone wants to get in touch with you – well, they just keep that ringer going and it's a pest! I thought you wanted to talk to me, or that you were in trouble, perhaps." I was aware that he was studying my reaction. "I can see you aren't conscious of it, but believe me, you have been bugging me!"

"Oh, Chen, I'm so sorry! As a matter of fact I did want to talk to you and - well, let's get home. Do you have a little time?"

It was a valuable visit. He told me he was aware that I had difficulties but that it was wrong to interfere or offer help unless asked. He told me he could advise me, but said he would like first to do an astrological reading to see what limits I was able to operate within.

"Astrology, you know, is a science," he told me. "It's nothing to do with fortune telling. Used properly it can help a person to make the most of their assets and deal with their defects, bring out the best in them, in other words. You could regard your life as a map; you are going to travel from A to B during your lifetime and you are going to meet obstacles along the way. Through astrology you can know the best route to take to get from A to B, how to avoid or deal with the pitfalls, what your limits are, at what point in your life things are likely to happen, good things as well as bad.

"We come to crossroads sometimes where we have to choose one path or the other. They both lead to B, but which is the best road to take? I believe you are at a crossroads, and you don't know which way to go." He took a sip of tea. He loved tea, and in all the years I was to know him he drank nothing other than tea or water. He was very middle of the way in most things, but alcohol he was completely opposed to. Being psychic he could actually see how alcohol can drive out the psyche in much the same way as hallucinatory drug use does, sometimes causing almost irreparable damage to the psyche.

Before he left, I promised I would talk to my mother and get the exact time of day that I was born so he could set up the chart accurately, or more or less so. He told me that in Tibet an astrolger would work out the details from the time of conception, but here - well, anyone's guess goes. In other words, the time and date of conception are seldom known.

Chen really had enough on his mind without my problems. He had known from the start that the book would not be without trouble, but he had known, too, that he would achieve his goal which was to make enough money from the book to get on with his research. He felt that the publisher personally trusted him. He felt that the agent did, too. At the same time, he knew about 'the old boy's club' and how hard it was if you were not a member, and he quite definitely had no wish at all to belong, he realized he was an outsider. When there were negative forces lurking around it made it that much more difficult to write as he wanted to write, each day was a battle, and walking home that morning, all this was on his mind. Others in the astral with whom he consulted were helpful but unless one was actually here on the Earth, actually experiencing firsthand, it was wellnigh impossible for them to visualize his problems.

Then he thought about me. I had asked him for guidance, and according to his belief he was bound to comply because he knew that he knew. He was bound to offer help, he could not just turn his back. But he had a strong suspicion that it was going to complicate his own life, and he had more than enough to contend with at the moment. He would have to talk to Ra'ab. She would not be in favour of helping anyone in the way he knew they would need to if he took me on, he was pretty sure of that, it would be too time consuming, for one thing, and she would see it as opening a can of worms, which in a way it was. She had a stake in his auric research, and would hate to see him distracted from that. He would have to point out the advantages to her, and there were always advantages if you knew how to make things work. After they had finished supper that evening, he brought it up. "I've promised to do an astrological chart for Sheelagh, just waiting for the time of birth from her mother. Do you want to help me with it?"

Chen invariably drew up the chart when he was doing a reading, but

Ra'ab often read it first, leaving him to check her reading afterwards. She had a good intellect and had made a thorough study of astrology. He, because he was psychic, was able to see more from a chart than the average astrologer, but he felt it wrong to disclose things not normally visible except to a psychic, which was the reason he liked Ra'ab to do the initial reading. In that way, information beyond the normal need not be disclosed.

She was busy at the sink, and without turning round she said, "Why are you doing a reading for her? Did she ask you to?"

"No, she didn't ask, I suggested it." He knew he had a fiery temper which he generally kept under good control, but Ra'ab could be devilishly irritating at times, dour, lacking in enthusiasm. It was hardly surprising that her first husband had found life too difficult, and had given up before finishing the job he was supposed to do. He sighed. "Sheelagh's at a crossroads and needs help. Who else can she turn to? And don't forget, she has helped us."

"Umm, and what do you think will happen to her if you don't help? A woman in her position must have plenty of friends without us."

"Her friends won't be there when she needs them, at least that's my impression. I think her life as she knows it now is going to end. I don't know, that's why I want to see her chart. But things are going to change drastically for her and subconsciously she knows it. She's afraid. She could have a breakdown. I probably am the only one who could help her avoid it. I can't stand aside and see her life ruined, that's part of the price one pays for 'seeing,' you know that."

Ra'ab took a book and propped herself up on her bed. She knew he would do what he had to do anyway, so what was the point of arguing. From the other side of the screen she said, "Well, let's hope it doesn't cause you too much trouble, that's all."

* * *

It must have been a week or perhaps ten days after that that I woke suddenly one night. I had no idea what time it was, but the house was silent and still. I got out of bed and went up to check on the children. They were sleeping like angels. I wondered where Chester was. Often he slept in the kitchen in his basket beside the warm Aga, and then would come upstairs to our bed in the early hours of the morning. I went quietly downstairs, hoping not to waken John, through the dining room and into the kitchen. There the old fellow was lying in his basket, but instead of rousing at my entry his body was still. I knelt beside him, and saw that he was not breathing. I put my ear to his heart. His body was still warm but there was no sign of life. He had died in his sleep, mercifully, without pain or bother.

My beloved and most constant companion who had seen me through the end of school, my engagement and marriage, the birth of our two children and my motherhood, who had been there for the ups and downs, the joys and sorrows, the sunlight and shadows, the friend who knew all, who was my comfort and prop, had left. I sat there in the kitchen with him until break of day and rigor mortis set in.

Later on that day, we wrapped him in his blanket and placed him in a wooden box. We buried him at the foot of the garden under an apple tree. Fenella stood silent and white, frozen with her grief. In her mind she was grappling with the mystery and power of death, and its inevitability. As John finished shovelling the earth, Jarvis brought Chester's drinking bowl filled with clean water from the garden tap, and placed it beside the grave. "When his ghost comes, Mama, it'll need a drink," he said earnestly. "Do you think we should leave a bone?"

"Don't be silly, Jarvis," snapped Fenella, "he's dead." And the tears overflowed from within her, ran down her cheeks and nose and into her open mouth as she cried.

I took both children by the hand, and we all slowly walked back to the house for tea. I felt, somehow, that a chapter of my life was nearing its end. I could not know it then, but it would be over twenty years before another dog entered my life. He was one of those 'small brown and white spaniels, playful, affectionate little creatures, pretty too,' that Martie had told us about, a Blenheim Cavalier King Charles spaniel. He was worth waiting for and I named him Beauvoir, or Beau to those who knew him.

CHAPTER FOUR

Most painters take a canvas and make a rough overall sketch first of what they have in mind, and then they proceed to paint, working the picture up all over the canvas, not just a corner at a time. It seems a logical way to go about it. But with magic painting it works quite differently. And when it is an imaginary magic painting as mine is - well, it works differently again. I wet the imagined paper a small bit at a time, then I watch in my mind as the colours and shapes appear, trying to put it into words. After that I go on to the next section.

The section we have arrived at now is cast in deep shadow, and it looks as though a cloud is passing over the sun, but there is no harm in that. There has to be balance in order for life to go on, and to achieve balance dark is as necessary as light, bad as necessary as good, sorrow as necessary as joy. In religion, to have the concept of God we need the devil in all his terrible glory. To have white we need black. Hitting the perfect balance is the only difficult part, and at times that can be extremely tiresome to achieve. Think, though, how impossibly exhausting it would be to have joy and sunshine all the days of our lives. So to experience a dark patch is actually not a bad thing at all. It balances out. At any rate, I have no intention of lingering too long over this particular dark area in my magic painting, I am not planning to try to peer through the cloud and analyze it all as a psychiatrist would do. It is important, though, to see some of it in order to give continuity to the story, and to explain how I came to live with the Rampa's in the first case.

It goes back to early childhood when the first hint was given that a big change would occur in my life. It must have made an impression because

I can remember it vividly, all the details. I can recapture that day, even the conversation and the dress of the people involved. I cannot say that I thought of it every day afterwards because I did not, but it was there in my subconscious and occasionally, through the years, surfaced into consciousness.

I had a great-aunt, my maternal grandmother's sister, who was fey. According to my down-to-earth, sensible, as most Victorians were, Scottish grandfather she was touched, not quite right in the head, and he was a doctor so he should know. He had no great opinion of his wife's family, they were too otherworldly for his taste. Actually, Auntie Jeannie, although she was a spinster, was sweet and delightful, gentle and pretty, but she had a certain habit of suddenly coming out with things that she felt were going to happen, and almost always they did. My mother was secretly quite fascinated with this ability of Auntie Jeannie's and would surreptitiously question her, ask her to read her palm, and then would say afterwards, "Of course it's all nonsense," while taking it quite seriously. My mother swung between her practical father, and her artistic, spiritualistic mother, on the surface favouring her father.

I remember quite clearly, although it must be over seventy years ago, Auntie Jeannie inviting us to tea this particular day in her neat little house in Harrogate. There were my mother, my brother, myself and some other people, grown-ups, I am not sure who they were, but they were sort of bookish and a little intimidating to a child. The house smelled of lavender and china tea, if a house can smell like that, china tea being so mild, but that was my impression. The maid, in her black frock and crisp white apron with a frilly and becoming white cap on her head, wheeled in the tea on a trolley covered by a heavy lace cloth. Then she returned with a mahogany stand, four tiers, and each with a plate of little bought cakes, which she placed close to my great-aunt before withdrawing. We had homemade cakes at home, so these seemed quite special with their coloured icing and intricate shapes. The cups were so fine you could see through them, but I was given a tumbler with milk.

The grown-ups were discussing the film of 'King Solomon's Mines' starring Paul Robeson which was currently on in Harrogate, when suddenly Auntie Jeannie turned to my mother and said, "My dear, John will always be there to look after you, he'll take care of you when you are an old, old lady." John was my brother and he did seem to manage my mother's ways much better than I ever did.

"Oh, well, that's very nice, but what about Sheelagh?" my mother replied, a little taken aback. It was expected that daughters would be more inclined to look after aged mothers than sons.

My great-aunt gazed at me in a vague sort of way. "Sheelagh? Oh, she won't be there." She beckoned for me to come to her chair and sit on the footstool beside her. I was ridiculously shy, and being the focus of attention was akin, in my mind, to what hell must be like, nevertheless, I crossed the room and sat down beside her. She took her gold pince-nez, which hung on a mauve silk ribbon round her neck, and adjusted them on her straight, delicate nose. Then, taking my hands in hers, she turned them palms up. "That's right," she repeated, as she looked at my hands, "she won't be there."

Afterwards, of course, I was forbidden to believe anything Auntie Jeannie said, it was complete and utter nonsense. But I never forgot it. I would look at my hands, and when I had some understanding of which line meant what, I could not help noticing that my life line on the left hand was chopped in three quite distinctly. Was I going to have a romantic early death? But no, that could not be it, the life line on the right hand was complete and unbroken, extending right around the thumb. Later on I purchased a book on chiromancy and pretended to read girls' hands at school, really to have a reason to look at their life lines, but I never saw another the same as mine, although there must be lots of people with a similar configuration. I just happened never to come across one. But I did decide that Auntie Jeannie's prediction that I 'wouldn't be there,' and the fact of the broken life line were tied together in some way, so that even if I was not dead, I would be somewhere other than with my family. The whole point is that I always knew I would, at some point, be making a big change, and would not be there. And the way it happened was like this:

My horoscope had been done and explained to me, all the ins and outs, all the possibilities, the limits I was able to operate within. A horoscope is quite a fascinating thing, and if it is explained properly can be very helpful.

It was not difficult to see, even without the horoscope, that things were not too brilliant in my life just then. It was explained that I was at a crossroads, but I was confused and unsure which way to go. I could continue on the same path and suffer nervous disorders, frustration and disaster in the sense of probable confinement, or I could take a completely different path and face criticism and rejection by family and friends. It appeared like a choice between the devil and the deep blue sea, but in fact, once I had resolved the dilemma, it was not. I was reminded of the vivid dream I had had in which Chester was talking to me, and I was reminded of my first encounter with Chen. Gradually the knowledge became clear to me that I was already on the path leading to a change, I became aware that that choice would lead to greater spiritual advancement than I could ever otherwise hope to achieve in this life.

The opinion of others was of no great importance in the real scheme of things. My children? Whichever route I was to follow I would be separated from them.

John had taken the children down to his parents' place in the country, and had spent the weekend there himself. We thought a holiday in the country would be pleasant for them, good for the grandparents, too, time alone with their grandchildren - well, not really alone because they had found a nanny, but that was as alone as they would ever be with them, at least while they were little. It was a Monday evening, I remember, and John must have gone straight to the office when he had arrived back in London that morning. I had not seen him since the previous Friday. I was sitting in the drawing room reading when I heard him come in. I pictured him removing his bowler, straightening his tie and smoothing his hair in the hall looking glass. Then I heard his step on the polished hall floor. He was in the room.

"Hello, darling, would you like a glass of sherry?" He bent down and kissed the top of my head casually as he spoke. Poor man, he had probably had a tiring day, I should not have sprung it on him like I did, but it was done before I thought.

"No, thanks, John, I'm not drinking. I'm going away for a time."

"Oh yes, sorry, I forgot. What's that?" he crossed to the corner cupboard to get a glass. "What did you say? You're going away? Where are you going?" He was pouring himself a stiff Scotch.

"I need a change, I think. I'm going to spend a little time with the Rampa's, you know, in their new flat. It's quite near here and there's lots of space. I don't feel well. I want to get better."

Silence, shocked silence. Then he said, "What do you want to stay with them for? Why don't you go to your parents?"

"No, no, John, don't be silly. That's the last thing I'd do, and I don't want them to know where I am, they'd just come ferreting around."

He was sitting in his chair opposite mine. He took out his cigarette case and lighter. "You're so odd, Sheelagh. It's hard to understand you."

I bit my lip. Yes, I knew I was odd, especially by his standards. Perhaps that was the trouble. "I know. I know it's hard for you. But John, take care of the children, take care of them, you will, won't you?"

"Of course, but you don't need to get so worked up. When are you going?"

"I thought I'd go this evening, you know, get it done, better sooner than later."

He nodded. "If that's what you want." He picked up his glass and stared into it for a few moment. "If that's what you really want."

"Yes, that's what I want."

It is strange how life's major moves are sometimes played out so fast, just a few words, just a few minutes, and everything changes. But that was how it was. And that was how I came to live with the Rampa's in the first case. It was not intended to be permanent, but as it turned out it endured for more than twenty years.

Around the time when I went to stay with them, the book was at a temporary standstill. Chen was being challenged by people who believed themselves experts on his country and beliefs. He was finding it difficult because these people appeared to be predisposed to dislike him. He was called upon to justify himself, but the thoughts of his challengers, and the actual dislike they displayed towards him, made it harder to deal with them. Although he had had no desire to write a book, since he was, in fact, doing it he was fully prepared to share his knowledge freely. Throughout the time I knew him, it was always his wish to take esoteric knowledge out of the realms of esoteric – or select – and make it available to anyone who was interested in learning. It was not knowledge that belonged to some elite club or group of intellectuals. It was basic, vital knowledge for everyone, and his style of writing was for everyone. The criticism and disbelief he faced wounded him profoundly, and made him cautious and appear to be solitary, it made him shut himself in, as sensitive people will do to protect themselves. The outcome of the business with the experts, however, was that they were completely unable to agree with each other, and the publisher, being confounded, decided to ignore them, which was a very wise move on his part.

During the time we lived in the first flat together there were two important happenings; the first was that 'The Third Eye' was finally published in the English language. It was an overnight success, and exceeded the dreams of Cecil Banks and the publisher, too. Before long, countries all over the world were seeking translation rights, practically all the European countries, Argentina, Japan, India, and, of course other English speaking countries like Canada, South Africa, Australia and the United States. Its publication changed our lives dramatically.

The second event that occurred was the birth of my third child, and I have to admit that I was so taken up with myself that the book's publication took second place in my mind.

A short time after leaving John and going to live with the Rampa's I went one afternoon to see my dressmaker, Madame D. I had a coat on order and, thinking I would hardly need it, my intention was to cancel the order but pay for any work that had gone forth. She was unusually and overly bright and charming, rather too talkative, uneasy. I deduced that she must have known I had left home and was embarrassed, but nevertheless we reached an amicable agreement and I took my leave of her somewhat sadly, I have to say. I would not be in need of pretty clothes for some time to come, if ever, I realised. Besides, I liked Madame D.

After leaving her, I decided to slip into Benedict's on the corner of Bond Street, a nice little place, low ceilinged and elegant, where they served large cups of chocolate coffee accompanied by wooden platters covered with a fig leaf, and on the fig leaf rested tempting morsels to nibble. It was a place frequented by smart shoppers, and was done up to please them. I had finished and was preparing to leave, when I caught sight of two women whom I knew entering the place. They were busy chatting and failed to see me, but they sat down close to where I was, with their backs towards me. Not really wishing to meet them, I hesitated before getting up to leave. They were still talking.

Roberta was a ringleader type, she was that kind of person, and she had that kind of carrying voice. "My dear, did you hear about Sheelagh? No?"

This was going to be interesting. I stayed put. She paused and I guessed the other one, Jane, was shaking her head. Roberta continued in a lower, super-charged voice, the type of voice you use when you have juicy news to impart, something hot off the press. "Well - and I got this from Cordelia so it must be true." She paused again for even greater effect. "She's left John!"

"Good lord! No! Really, how extraordinary. Has she run off with that young David who's always mooning around after her?" Jane was incredulous, but all the same fascinated.

"No, no, my dear, much worse than that, MUCH worse. You'll never believe it, you really won't." Another pregnant pause. "She's gone off with some sort of yogi, or something. He's written a book, apparently."

"Good Lord! Amazing! A yogi? One of those natives who sit around naked?! Poor John. She must have gone completely mad. It must be the pregnancy. She's nearly due, isn't she?"

"Yes, but then, you know, John only married her on the rebound after that affair with the bishop's daughter - you know, Sally," said Roberta with authority. "You remember, old Ma Rouse was really cut up when she jilted him, the Church and all that, right up her street for a daughter-in-law. Never approved of Sheelagh, you know. Of course, she was just a child when he married her, didn't know a thing, probably still doesn't, come to that. Cordelia's going to dine out for weeks on this! She's so clever at taking people off." They both laughed.

"What about the children?" asked Jane.

"Oh, I'm told they're in the country with Ma Rouse. She's got a sensible nanny for them. They'll be so much better off. Sheelagh ruined them, hasn't a clue about discipline. Poor girl, they'll probably lock her up in one of those asylums when she comes back. It's the only thing to do with those sort of cases."

At that point the waitress tripped up to their table and they started to give their order. I got up and turned to walk out of the place, passing them as I went. Deliberately I stopped beside their table. "Roberta, Jane, how nice to see you both! I thought you would be in the country like everyone else!" I bestowed my best and most charming smile upon them.

Roberta looked at me, her eyebrows arched and her long aqualine nose twitching slightly, making her look more than ever like an overbred race horse.

"My dee-aa-rr," she drawled, "how delightful, we were just saying we hadn't seen you for absolutely ages, weren't we Jane, absolutely ages."

Jane was busy with her gloves, barely looking at me. Then she glanced up and said, "Oh, yes, that's right, we haven't seen you for ages, absolutely ages." She gave what passed for a smile, looking at me through her pert little eye veil. I almost felt sorry for her, poor girl, poor, poor girl. It was laughable. "And how are those darling children?" she went on, recovering herself a little.

"So far as I know, doing very well.," I told her. "Sensible nannies and mothers-in-law know how to do it, don't they? But, incidentally, Roberta, you've got it a bit wrong, you know. The word is not 'yogi.' It's 'lama,' with one 'l' to distinguish it, you know, from the long necked creature that roams around in the Andes, or somewhere. What? You don't know what a lama is? My dear, you should read the book, it's called 'The Third Eye.' Everyone's reading it. Now I really must fly. Lovely to see you both." I made for the door without a backward glance. I walked up Bond Street to catch a bus home. Although I felt I had won that round, there would be dozens of others I would probably never even know about. So what did it matter? They could all go to hell, for all I cared, and good riddance. All the same, I did feel a bit rattled and out of sorts, not quite right somehow. They really were incredibly horrible, those two women. I loathed them both at that moment quite heartily.

As I sat on the bus I began to wish I had taken a taxi. The bus was so jolty, so slow, it seemed that the whole of Oxford Street was blocked with traffic. I began to be sure the baby was imminent, I just had that feeling. I was supposed to be going to a hospital for the birth, but was not looking forward to it. I had never been in a hospital before.

When I arrived home I went straight to my room and lay down on the bed. It was not long before Ra'ab appeared at the door with a cup of tea. They must have sensed something was wrong. "Are you all right?" she asked.

"I don't know. I have a feeling the baby is on the way. Can we send for the doctor?"

"I'll get Chen to come and look at you, but we'll send for a doctor right away if you like. There may not be time to get you to hospital."

She was a nurse and he was a doctor, so they were calm, experienced . Chen came and looked at me, then he placed his hands with the palms over my eyes and his fingers spread over my head. He told me to relax, and I felt an indescribable peace and calm flood my mind. It was as though there were no worries, it was as though I had been given some marvellous gift which allowed me to see above and beyond, to get away from pain and the confines of the flesh. I felt free and happy.

It was in that state of mind that my third child, a boy, was born not very long after, and I can remember nothing difficult about it. Ra'ab had contacted a doctor and a midwife, but the latter did not arrive until after the birth, the doctor arriving a few hours later. It was Chen who brought the child into the world, who washed him and wrapped him in warm clothes.

As I turned and heard the child utter his first cry, I distinctly saw a golden glow around Chen's head. That was the first and only time I saw it during all the years I was to know him, and I put it down to the fact that I was in an altered state and able to see what normally I would not have seen. To my understanding, it was the nimbus, or higher force possessed by advanced entities, and not the same thing as the aura which we all possess and which is composed of lines of force such as a magnet has around it, but of different colours, more colours than we are capable of seeing unless clairvoyant.

What I saw that day was what one would call the halo. Curiously, or perhaps not so curiously, my second son, while resembling John physically, is endowed with exceptional insight and awareness, and his lifestyle today is one to which I have aspired but never achieved. I am convinced that the first moments of life are vital to an individual's development, and somehow set a pattern for the life ahead, like an indelible stamp on the blueprint of life.

* * *

It was a cold, dismal day of midwinter, already late afternoon and past time to turn on lights and draw curtains when John arrived for his third visit. He came unannounced and found me resting, the three week old baby, whom we had decided to name Khanda, in his cradle beside my bed. He took a cursory look at the baby (at that age beauty truly lies in the eyes of the beholder), then removed his black crombie overcoat, casually throwing it across the foot of my bed. I remained resting, my head on the large square pillow, as I watched him. He took the big easy chair, which seemed to accommodate him well. It was covered with dark red velvet, the kind that never ever wears out, and must have been on that chairs for years, it must have had scores of people sitting on it, it retained a faint, not unpleasant smell of tobacco, cigars, I would say. It just had that smell of a certain kind of well-to-do family, solid, unshakeable, the kind of family that also goes on for years and years just like the chair, indestructible. It suited my husband.

I got up and crossed to the window to draw the curtains across and shut out the night. I clicked the switch of the small lamp beside my bed, hoping not to disturb the baby. We said nothing. As I resumed my resting position John got out his silver cigarette case and offered it to me.

"No, thanks, John." We were always polite, but his inability to remember my not smoking or drinking when pregnant or breast feeding was infuriating. I continued to watch him as he lit his cigarette, so complacent, so privileged, so well dressed and composed. I knew then that I could never return to him, I knew his life was not for me. He stifled me, and he, for his part, must have felt immense annoyance towards me, although he seldom showed it. He was superbly restrained.

Eventually he spoke, "Darling, do you have any idea what you want to do? I think we have to make some decision about the child for one thing. Nanny is marvellous, the children love her, they've never been better. She'd adore a baby to take care of. Easier for you. I don't think you're well enough to look after him. You have to think of yourself, you know, you have to take care not to overdo it."

"I don't know what you mean. I'm not sick or anything!" I was defensive.

"Mmm, do you have an ashtray?" He was treating me with caution.

"Look, John, I'll have to think about it. I know it's hard for you. I know you find me difficult." I was desperately trying to be reasonable, but to make a decision of that kind immediately was impossible. "I'll telephone you tomorrow, I need to sleep on it."

When he left, he kissed me gently on the forehead. He had never told me he loved me, and there is no reason to suppose that he did, yet I was the mother of his children, I had taken care of them and of him, and for that he was grateful.

The next day I rang him up and told him I was not returning, and Khanda should be taken to the bosom of the family where he would grow up with the privileges his birth accorded him. I had no clear idea of my own future, but I felt it did not include money or position or worldly security of any kind. I had no wish for those things any more. Did I ever regret that decision? Yes, I feel sure that from time to time I did, probably more often than I actually remember because one tends to block out memories one finds unpleasant. Sometimes, I may have felt unable to manage the path I had chosen. But at the end of the day, in other words, now – no I have no regrets. I stayed the course and I think I learned from it. In my belief, what we learn in life is what we take back to our Overself when we leave the physical body in death, so, ultimately, that is what counts, that is what it is all about.

* * *

When people read a book that impresses them they often feel the urge to write to the author. Chen received a great many letters from a wide variety of readers. He read them all. They would be forwarded on from the publisher and would arrive, usually with an elastic band around them because there were a lot. Methodically he would slit open the envelope with his paper knife, examining the writing. As he read the letters he would place them in piles, these required a short acknowledgement only, those required thought and a detailed answer, others asked for and needed no response. Obviously, he preferred the latter! It was a heavy workload and for a time he did it almost single-handed, that is to say, Ra'ab addressed envelopes, folded the letters and posted them.

It was not until Khanda had gone to live with his father and siblings that I became involved with the letters, and I was at such a loose end then that I was thankful to have something to do. In a way, it grew on me and gradually, over many years, and as Chen had to write more books as well as pursue his research, it fell to me to take a large role in dealing with the fan mail.

He always opened letters, read or scanned them according to their importance and need, then handed them to me and we discussed his reply. Sometimes he would dictate a reply, at others he would simply indicate the gist or say, "You know what to say." It was an interesting experience, like having a crowd of acquaintances you never met, but because they often wrote very frankly of their problems and lives in general, you came to know them thoroughly. It was a unique lesson in humanity, and one I enjoyed and benefitted from. As well, I learned a great deal in an indirect fashion from Chen's replies to involved questions relating to occult and metaphysical matters. I came to respect the readers who already were possessed of significant knowledge, who were deeply spiritual and often lived modest lives. I was fascinated by the number of people who had had spiritual, esoteric experiences and were writing, not only to relate their experiences, but also because they may not have fully understood them. I loved the gentleness and unworldliness of so many who wrote. I loved and appreciated the understanding of so many intelligent individuals. Unavoidably, there were those whom we labelled "crackpot mail", but there were surprisingly few of those; perhaps they were not sound mentally and were ready to latch onto anything out of the ordinary. We treated them with tact, if replying at all, but with finality.

Contrary to popular belief, I was never a student sitting at Chen's feet, ingesting esoteric knowledge. I learnt in a different and perhaps more thorough way. What I know is what over the years I absorbed from him. It was not the kind of learning possessed, for instance, by academics who are taught with the idea that they be able to discuss what they know in a scholarly fashion. What they learn and what they are able to discuss does not necessarily become a part of them, it may well remain only in the conscious mind - and we are only one-tenth conscious. On the other hand, erudition which has been absorbed, or which has 'rubbed off' unconsciously through contact with an Adept, may not be something one can discuss in a scholarly manner, yet it is knowledge that has become deeply ingrained into the subconscious, it becomes a permanent part of one's inner knowing.

If you look up the word metaphysics in the dictionary you will see that it is described as, 'The science and causes of all things existing. The philosophy of mind as distinguished from that of matter.' And if you wonder exactly what a psychic person is, that could be defined as one who is aware of multi-dimensional worlds, not just our three dimensional world, one who can see and experience what normal three dimensional people cannot. In the same way to make it perhaps a little more clear, a normal human being who is three dimensional can see and experience what an amoeba which is one dimensional cannot. The knowledge and understanding I gained during the years I spent with Chen could come under the heading of those two words, metaphysics and psychic.

Many people wonder about many things, but one of the main questions was about the Akashic Record. What is it? Who can see it?

The Akashic Record is the record of everything that has ever happened impressed on the ether in much the same way as light impulses are recorded on cine film. In the astral state it is possible to see what you want to see on that Record, just as now we can see things on the Internet. (The Internet, however, is completely different from the Akashic in that it consists only of what people have entered into it, not necessarily true facts, while the Akashic is a record of what actually has occurred.)

And the Akashic Record of Probabilities can perhaps be best explained in this way: Imagine a train on a track as seen from above, as seen from a balloon or an aeroplace high above the earth. From that vantage point, it is possible to see the track ahead, and one may see that the train is headed for a crash because the points are not set correctly. But it is not a definite fact until it has happened because someone might come along in the nick of time and set the points so that the train will pass over that potentially dangerous bit of track, and arrive on time in good shape. So the Akashic Record of Probabilities is a good indication of just that - probabilities.

It would be wrong to give the impression that psychics sit around and look at the Akashic Record as people sit around and watch television, often mindlessly. Even with psychic ability, it requires knowledge and energy to get far enough into the astral to be able to consult the Akashic in the way that Chen was able to do.

At that time, the period when 'The Third Eye' was published, there were numerous negative forces actively attempting to disrupt and cause annoyance to him, and Chen had to be mindful of it all in order to combat it. The reader will be aware by now that he was focussed only on getting his task connected with the human aura completed. That was his aim and purpose, everything else was secondary, and every move he made was towards that goal. His life was conducted as a game of chess, and his moves were made with care and forethought. He considered his work of importance to the human race, and thus to the universe. There were few people capable of doing it, and he intended to remain alive until that work was accomplished. So it was that he needed to be left entirely alone at night. I was asked never to disturb him because he travelled far, far out of the body in the astral state, attached to the physical body, as we all are, by the Silver Cord, and a sudden disturbance could bring him back too abruptly, it could even cause death, or, at the best, a severe headache and nausea. At that time he would appear white and drawn in the morning and the site of the pineal gland, or the 'third eye' in the centre of the forehead, would be angry red and sore looking. We would know he had been consulting with others in the astral. Sometimes he talked about it, at other times he remained silent, and one knew better than to question him.

As one example of the negative forces I just mentioned, we had a visit from two Scotland Yard detectives during the time we lived in the London flat together. I remember the day distinctly because Ra'ab had been out to buy herself a dress, and we had had discussions about where she should shop. She ended up at Jaegar in Regent Street, and came home with a charming blue tweedy dress which suited her admirably. She had tried it on to show us and was still wearing it when Chen, who was in his customary place by the window, suddenly exclaimed, "Ah, here they are at last!"

"Here who are?" I asked, as I crossed the room to join him at the window.

"You see those two men," he indicated a pair of men with homberg hats pulled well down over their eyes and wearing identical raincoats, walking closely side by side.

Ra'ab had come to the window. "They look like police," she said. It was a fact, they looked exactly like the cops in the cops and robber films that excited us as children and they had a kind of gliding more than walking movement about them.

"That's just what they are, policemen," Chen said. "I've been expecting them. They're coming here." He got up. "I'll put my jacket on in honour of them. Police don't like anything different, especially when dealing with foreigners." He was making light of it, as he always did, but even so one knew how distasteful and difficult these situations were for him. It is bad enough for a non-psychic person to be interviewed by police, but for a psychic - it must be quite dreadful to see into their minds. He was wearing a comfortable saffron coloured robe made by Ra'ab when he was photographed for book publicity. He liked the robe and had taken to wearing it in the house instead of his suit, but now he was going to change into his jacket to appear more conventional.

The two men disappeared from our view as they neared the building. I was alarmed. Police meant trouble of some sort, even if one is as innocent and pure as the driven snow, there is still a feeling of alarm when a policeman arrives at the door! When the bell rang and they did indeed announce themselves as being from Scotland Yard, I would go so far as to say it was a frightening experience. But they were courteous and after a brief visit left, satisfied. It transpired that they were investigating a complaint that Chen was running an unregistered nursing home. Was it not true that a child had been born here in this very place recently? Who was the child, where was the mother, what was the explanation?

"I'm sorry, Sheelagh, it's your parents. They don't like me. They'll make trouble as long as they can," Chen told me. I was mortified. I felt responsible for the trouble he was having to face, but there was nothing to be done. It was amazing to me then, as I still was not fully aware of Chen's abilities, that he knew the police were on the war path. He laughed, "I don't just write about things, you know," he said.

Apart from that experience, life in London was beginning to be difficult. Chen had become too well known and sought after to be able to remain as private as he wished – and needed – to be. He decided that we should move to a quieter place, and somewhere where perhaps the taxes would not be so exorbitant for writers as they were in England. There were few choices, and eventually we decided to move to Ireland, to Dublin. It turned out to be a good choice. It was the beginning of one of the best periods for Chen's work. He made progress with research, he continued to write, the atmosphere and close proximity to the sea were very conducive to psychic work.

We answered an advertisement which was brief and to the point: 'Furnished flat to rent, central Dublin,' and took the place sight unseen. This was the first of many, many moves over the next twenty years or so, and it was actually one of the most pleasant and successful for us all.

CHAPTER FIVE

Generally speaking preconceived notions about places and people lead to grand disillusionment. But such was not the case with Ireland. It is hard to say now where my notions had originated, and I can only assume it was from books we read as small children, and perhaps, also, from our maternal grandmother's collection of old Irish silver and the stories she attached to each piece. She was an imaginative woman.

My brother and I were what you might call precocious, or advanced, readers. Then there was no television. We read a great deal, and books at that time were almost works of art. It was a truly tactile experience to hold a well bound book, usually beautifully illustrated, in one's hands. We graduated quickly from the bedtime stories our mother read to us at a tender age, going on to reading to ourselves while still very young, before we went to school even. With her we had agonized, gloried and shivered through 'The Lancashire Witches,' on to Greek mythology, neither of which ensured a peaceful night's rest. By the time we were able to bury our heads in our own books we had acquired quite a sense of literature; my brother would be engrossed in 'Stalkey & Co,' 'Treasure Island,' 'The Scarlet Pimpernel', or the adventures of Dick Hanney, while I was sculling down the river with Ratty, following Alice and the white rabbit with pink eyes down the rabbit hole, or riding on Nana's back with the Darling children.

So where did the Irish stories come in? Well, for one there was a wonderful book, a large book it was, I can almost see it now, thick paper and every so often a marvellously graphic picture of faeries, goblins, and leprechauns, odd little fellows with tall hats. And there were tales of tinkers and donkeys, ruined castles shrouded in mist. It was enchanting. I loved it and I lived it, although for the life of me I cannot remember its title. And then, of course, there was Irish poetry, romantic, magical stuff that went round and round in one's head leading to serious daydreaming and 'lack of attention' when forced to go to school, where I sat at the back enveloped in a mystical land of castles and leprechauns.

Our grandmother's Irish silver and the stories that went with it only added to the romance of the place. Why she collected Irish silver is a mystery. It may have been an oblique method of causing annoyance to my grandfather who was Scottish - she herself being from Yorkshire - or it may simply have been that Irish silver was hard to come by so the challenge of collecting it was far greater. What made it even more of a challenge was that she favoured women silversmiths, and there were fewer of the fair sex in the trade. Now I come to think of it, it seems to me that our grandmother must have been a forerunner of the Women's Liberation Movement, heavily disguised. Like her sister, my Great Aunt Jeannie, the one who was fey, she was petite and delicate in appearance, and she used lily-of-the-valley toiletries; wherever Granny had been the elusive scent hung briefly and faintly in the air, attesting to her recent presence.

From Granny I learned about such women as Annie Nolan of Loughrea, County Galway, who was busily engaged in silversmithing around 1780. Granny owned a lovely chocolate pot with this lady's mark, along with the date and place marks, and I was made to feel it and then compare the feeling with modern machine made silver. Not the same thing at all. The former was like silk compared to the coarser touch of the latter. Then she had, and used daily, a wonderful tea set, quite ornate in fact, made by a

Dorothy Manjoy or, as she liked to tell everyone, really Mountjoy but pronounced Manjoy, because, as people were 'not terribly well educated in those days,' they would not have known how to pronounce the name correctly had it not been written as it was spoken. 'Those days' referred to the early 18th century, earlier than Annie Nolan, and Dorothy worked in Kilkenny. And there were others too, one who made buttons, and several from Dublin. They all had stories attached to them, made up, I feel sure, by Granny. She told about their houses, the clothes they wore, their husbands and children of which they seemed to have an astonishingly large number, leading one to question how they had time to ploy their craft.

"They were strong," Granny said with satisfaction.

All this was a positive beginning to a new life. Although I had no physical knowledge or acquaintance with Ireland, other than a friendship with an Irish girl at school for a time, I felt I knew where I was going, it was exciting and attractive. And I had the natural optimism and curiosity of youth on my side. As I contemplate my magic painting, the picture I am attempting to bring to life in words, the colours of this particular area are clear and bright, the shapes are well defined and the heavy dark clouds are giving way to lighter hues. It was a good time, at least for a while.

Our landlady in Dublin had a title and a bicycle. The latter was of far greater use to her than the former which carried little prestige and no wealth, but she did own and live in a castle in the Wicklow Mountains outside Dublin. The place was mostly in ruins, but it readily fulfilled my dreams of castles looming up out of the mist. The bicycle was quite splendid, a shiny black Raleigh with a red stripe, and it took her everywhere. Attached to the handlebars was a large wicker basket in which Ping, her aristocratic and cross pekinese dog rode. Pong, so she told us, had come to a sad and gory end only two years previously, and I liked to think, because I am inclined to give dogs the benefit of the doubt, that his untimely demise had contributed largely to Ping's displeasure with life in general.

Lady Shane, as was her name, invited me to tea not too long after we moved into the flat. Very little of the castle was habitable, but it was enough for herself and Ping, and for the aged retainer who seemed moulded into the place. We had scones and strawberry jam with big mugs of strong Indian tea, sitting in the kitchen with Maggie, the retainer, hovering in the background, and grumbling all the while under her breath about her legs.

The kitchen was huge and vaulted, the flagstoned floor worn by the passage of years and booted feet. The big black kettle that was used to boil water for our tea hung on a hook over the great open fire. There must surely have been a man about the place, for there was an enormous pile of logs stacked up beside the fireplace. I admired the table, although it was a puzzle to me, and she explained that her late husband had made it himself out of one of the stout old doors of the castle, saving it from decay. She showed me exactly where the hinges had been, and told how he had found six carved and claw-footed legs in a secondhand shop in Dublin and had lovingly made the whole into a table. She went on to tell me that he had been educated at Stoneyhurst, one of the two important Catholic public schools in England, but the family had had to scrape the bottom of the barrel in order to educate him. "He was a dreamer," she said with a shrug. If she thought his education was a waste, she gave no indication of it.

After tea we went out to inspect the garden. At one time it must have been quite beautiful, and its situation was breathtaking; the gentle rolling hills in the distance, the soft mist and the feeling of isolation and peace. She told me that her mother-in-law had been a keen gardener, "but she was English", which seemed to sum it all up. Now the garden, like the house, had fallen into neglect, and the unkempt grazing land beyond had encroached upon it.

The Shane property in Dublin in which we lived was similarly in need of repair, a fact which was a cause of annoyance to the Rampa's, although not in the least disturbing to me. Unlike myself, the aesthetic side of accommodation meant little to them mainly, I imagine, because they had been forced to live in sub-standard places through lack of money for too long. The flat we occupied comprised the top floor of the building and what I can only describe as a mezzanine, a single room which jutted out halfway up the stairs between the first and top floors of the place. This room was allotted to me, and I was charmed by it. On the ground floor was a florist's shop so there was always the welcome of cheerful colours and exotic scents when returning home from shopping or anything else. Climbing the narrow, rickety staircase one had to pass the tailor's establishment on the first floor before reaching my room half way up the next flight. The tailor was a genial enough fellow, his only failing being a predilection for bacon and sausage which comprised his daily lunch menu to judge by the aroma wafted up the stairs. But it is true, and must be said, there are worse things than bacon and sausage for lunch.

Lady Shane rode her bicycle in to Dublin to collect rent from us all regularly. She would arrive dressed in warm ancient tweeds, sturdy sensible shoes and stockings, and a felt hat rammed on her head and secured by two hat pins, lethal looking weapons, to combat the winds. Her ruddy, weather-worn cheeks and glowing nose were proof of her stalwart open air life. If it was wet, as it frequently was, although a friendly type of rain bestowing only health and beauty, she wore an all-enveloping mackintosh, and had had another cut for Ping from a discarded, older mackintosh. I had never, at that time, seen a dog so attired, although it is common now – even rain bootees these days – and I found it absurd and amusing to see his cross little face staring out from under the cover of his hooded raingear.

The advertisement for the flat had been so brief that no one could accuse it of being misleading, and, in any case, everyone has a conflicting idea of what furnished means. I can only say it was sparsely furnished, and what there was was not exactly pristine. However, it was tasteful and evoked a past era. I personally like old rugs even if they do smell rather of camels, I find big antiquated chairs comforting and pleasing, and I especially like old looking glasses - they are shameless flatterers. What perhaps upset Chen and Ra'ab most was that nearly all the plates, cups, saucers, everything, in fact, used for cooking and eating, was chipped, cracked, or warped in one way or another. They felt it was unhealthy and they found themselves obliged to buy new. It was incomprehensible to Lady Shane, causing her to see us as slightly mad.

The flat was situated right across the street from the grounds of Trinity College, and Chen found great pleasure in the library, not open to the public but he obtained a readers' pass to allow him the privilege of studying there whenever he pleased. The big windows upstairs looked out over the university grounds.

My mezzanine room had a long window to the floor with a flat roof outside. It was at the back of the building, and the flat roof was almost enclosed by two walls, the backs of other buildings. It gave to my room a cosy and private feeling. Early in the morning, as the first hints of dawn streaked across the sky, the seagulls would arrive and I would waken to their clawed feet, pitter pat, pitter pat, on the concrete roof as they sought out whatever prey the night prowling felines had left over from their excursions. A gull would grab a morsel, fight over it with others who had alighted as if summoned by telepathy, and the winner would rise in flight triumphantly with the others, screaming their primordial cry, in pursuit. I loved to hear the seagulls, the wildness of them, their freedom and in a certain way I envied them. A little later on, one would hear the clanging of church bells, calling the faithful to begin their day in piety, and then from somewhere nearby the sonorous chimes of a clock giving the hour, the quarter, the half or three-quarters. It all wove into a pattern, became habitual, the start of a new day in a new life. Life in Dublin was good. The Irish people had suffered great hardship and deprivation for centuries, and even now lived under the yoke of their religion, but somehow it had refined them and given a depth of understanding which a newcomer could pick up and appreciate. We all felt comfortable there.

It must have been around that time that I first became aware that Chen's work with the aura was actually rather more than the perfecting of a machine to view the aura for the medical profession, but I was not to fully realize the implications until much later. I was still at that time very much a novice in matters pertaining to higher esoteric lore.

Quite shortly after we moved to Dublin Chen and Ra'ab started to discuss finding models for auric photography. Apparently, the female aura is generally brighter than the male, the colours stronger, and so it was necessary to find women willing to pose nude. Ra'ab's view was that it would be virtually impossible, she saw the young Catholic women as being overly modest, and hesitated to even make enquiries. Chen, with a deeper knowledge of human nature, saw no such difficulty. "What about the girl in the flower shop? I imagine her pay is minimal. Doesn't she have a child to support? Ask her. There's no harm in asking. I'm willing to wager she'll be glad to have extra money." He was right. As it turned out, there was no shortage of models, nice girls for the most part who needed a little extra money. The photographic equipment required was also in supply, and he began to develop and print his own material when he was not using Polaroid cameras. We set up the bathroom as a dark room, and woe betide anyone who opened the door at the wrong moment and wrecked a film!

He was keen for me to take up photography, and showed me how to use quite complicated equipment. In those days it was more of a skill to use any kind of camera. Cameras such as we were using were not automatic, they were for the most part designed for expert professional use and it was necessary to use light meters and many different lenses. In his work he was making long exposures, so there were tripods and lights around for my use at all times. It was a hobby for me, and truthfully rather an enforced one, not something I ever became passionate about, but I did learn about different cameras, from minute spy cameras like the Gami and Minox, to large format cameras used by some of the wonderful original photographers, to the Hasselbad and modern Japanese cameras. And then to cine photography. My feeling is that Chen did make progress at that time, but he had no luck in obtaining specially sensitized film, which was what he really needed. The demand was not large enough for it to be a proposition for the big manufacturers.

As well as photography he began writing another book. Ra'ab and I would leave him alone for a couple of hours or so daily in order that he could dictate without fear of interruption. Often we would go out for dinner, although there were relatively few restaurants at that time in Dublin. Powers Hotel on the corner near to us was a favourite for their excellent soda bread and good plain food. The next day I would transcribe the tape using a Phillips machine and a manual Olympia typewriter, alone in my mezzanine room. It was fascinating. I sat there with a padded headset, listening, transcribing what I heard, often lost in the work. He dictated very clearly, never hesitating or backtracking. It was easy to type from his dictation, and he very seldom — in fact almost never – altered anything once he had dictated it.

In our daily life we were not in the least intense. Contrary to press reports and similar, we never had groups or indivduals for any form of psychic activity. We did not engage as a group in meditation, yoga or other extrasensory activities. Chen was the antithesis of a cultist. Naturally, he would perhaps uncover his crystal for some reason (normally it was kept on a stand covered with a square of black velvet), or he might ask us not to speak for a few minutes while he received a telepathic message, things like that. But in general, we discussed photography, Ireland, cats, the latest news, world events, subjects any reasonably intelligent people might discuss. So to be transcribing this highly intense material was a privilege.

It is true, as has been pointed out by those who enjoy criticism, that Chen had a perfect command of the English language, too perfect, they thought, for a Tibetan. It has also been said that his spoken English was that of a north country Englishman, a south country Englishman, a Londoner, and so on. But that is untrue. The fact of such a variety of opinions invalidates them anyway. It was not possible to place him from his manner of speech. The only deviation that I noticed, and teased him about, was that he would say 'boughten' instead of 'bought' occasionally. Since he could not hear, I always assumed that he had learned to speak the language from patterns he saw or felt. His spoken English transcended class and was intelligible to everyone. The problem is that normal, non-psychic people do not understand psychic ability, so we naturally judge the world by normal non-psychic standards. Our standards, though, are quite limited to a psychic who is endowed with much greater ability. Chen was as a sighted man in the land of the blind. How to explain to a normal person not endowed with psychic ability that he could learn a language from patterns and speak it as a native? Impossible, one cannot!

There are many psychic phenomena which are unexplainable in concrete language because there are no terms of reference. Those things have either to be taken on trust until one's inner self reaches realization – as happens – or one can simply keep an open mind. Regrettably, many choose to disbelieve because they are unable to take anything on trust or to keep an open mind.. That is perhaps why, despite his inner peace, Chen could still feel lonely and often did. At times, even, he felt miserable because he was misunderstood and very much alone. He was necessarily subject to lesser qualities, as we have to be in order to stay on this Earth. He never professed to be a saint. Even now I can almost hear his voice saying, so many times did I hear it, "The Middle Way is the only way. If you are too good you can't remain here, and its never a good idea to be too bad, it catches up on you!" One of his failings and one which worked against him was hypersensitivity.

He could take offense where none was intended. A good example and one which comes to mind is that of a famous American writer, a deep thinker, who had written in praise of 'The Third Eye.' At some point in their exchange of letters he had remarked that Chen was not religious. It was clearly a perceptive observation, a compliment meaning that he was above religion, his form of Buddhism was a Way of Life, not a religion. Sadly, however, he took offense and terminated the correspondence abruptly and without explanation.

* * *

"Chen, I'm so sorry, I can't wear a watch, they never go on me."

"Have you ever tried a gold one?"

"No."

"Well, try this one, I think it will work."

These mornings of my old age, so long after, sometimes I waken with thoughts or words in my mind, and I am taken back to that life, those years I lived with the Rampa's. It is as if time is non-existent. In my mind I am there again for a brief moment, that moment between sleep and wakefulness.

The watch, the old gold watch. Yes, I still have it, it still tells the time, it is still a treasured possession and, as he knew it would, it did keep time on my wrist as no other watch I had attempted to wear had done previously.

When we lived in Dublin we would sometimes rent a car for the day. We never drove too far afield, there was no need to, you could be out of the city in a matter of ten minutes or so. We would sometimes go up to the Wicklow Mountains, soft, mellow country, watercolour country, expressionistic with forms and colours melting into each other. At other times we would go along the coast, south to Dun Loaghlaire where the boats from Liverpool docked. Or we might go the other way to Sutton Cross and on to Howth, a large fishing village with the Bailey lighthouse on the point, mournfully wailing through the fog and flashing its light to alert sailors of their bearings, and warn of the rocky waters and their close proximity to land.

It was one of those days that Chen and Ra'ab had decided to take a ride with Ku'ei and I had elected to stay at home because I had plenty to do, letters to type as well as the book, and I hated to get behind with my work. It seemed they had been gone almost no time at all - or was it really that I was absorbed in what I was doing? - when I heard them going up the stairs past my door, Ku'ei with her Siamese cat voice telling the world she was glad to be home but she had had a splendid outing, Ra'ab asking her to be quiet, and then Chen's tread on the stair. The others went on, but he stopped outside my door and gently knocked. "May I come in?"

I got up, glad to see him. "But of course!" I turned my chair around so he could sit down. It was a firm chair, one I used for typing and quite comfortable for him for short periods of time. I sat on my bed, plumping up the pillows to make a cushion.

"Thank you, but I won't stay for long." He felt in his pocket and brought out a small black box. As he handed it to me, he said, "You've been working too hard, you need a change, but here's a little present until such time as we can get the book done and take a rest and a holiday."

I took the box and opened it. There nestling in a bed of green silk was a little gold watch. It was quite delightful. Without even lifting it out of the box I could tell it was old, the gold had that warm, reddish hue, and the face was clear and simple. Old things speak to one, and I instantly felt that the little watch was just right. But I was dismayed.

"Chen, I'm so sorry, I can't wear a watch, they never go on me." I was confused, not wishing to appear ungrateful, yet not wishing to accept something I felt unable to use.

"Have you ever tried a gold one?" he asked.

"No."

"Well, try this one. I think it will work." He smiled, seeing that I really loved the watch, as I took it out and held it in my hand. "Here, let's see if it's the right size for you."

He fastened the gold bracelet on my left wrist, and it was a perfect fit, just enough room for movement. He removed it again and compared the time with his own watch, setting the hands correctly and carefully winding it up. As he did so, he took the chair I had offered him, after all, and said, "It's a pity you can't do psychometry, you'd find it interesting, especially as you like old things so much."

"What do you mean by psychometry, Chen?" I was indeed interested.

"Well, someone who is psychic or sensitive can hold an object in their hand, and by letting the mind go blank the sub-conscious can activate para-normal senses so that the fingers can convey vibrations to the brain which form pictures. As I've told you many times," he continued, seeing I was listening intently, "all life is electric and magnetic, and anything that has been touched by a person always has the mark, or impression, of that person in future. It's like touching a piece of iron with a magnet, you partly magnetize that piece of iron. A galvanometer or a magnetic compass can detect the magnetism imparted to the iron. Do you follow?"

"Yes, I think so. You mean you're like the compass, in a way, when you do psychometry, you can detect the impressions."

"That's right. I can hold your watch in my hand like this," he had the watch resting in the palm of his hand as he spoke, "and by letting my mind go blank I can see pictures of events in the life of this object."

He closed his eyes, and sat silent for a few minutes. I hardly dared to breathe. I wanted to know about the little watch, and was afraid of putting him off the track. Presently he spoke, still with his eyes closed. "Yes, it belonged to a very elegant woman, French probably, or perhaps Italian, dark haired. She wore the watch constantly, valued it highly. When she was dying she gave it to another woman close to her, perhaps a servant or a nurse, someone she was rewarding, or thanking. The watch was put away for quite a long time, the other woman never wore it." He stopped speaking, but after a pause continued, "I can't get anything else just now."

"Oh, but that's fascinating!" I was delighted. I was determined to wear this watch, and see that it worked on my wrist. Perhaps in time I, too, would be able to see its past. He handed it back to me and I fastened the clasp securely. I knew it was right for me. "Thank you so much, Chen, it's so very kind and thoughtful of you. I shall value it as greatly as the woman you described, the original owner." I was sincere in my gratitude.

"Well, we're going to have tea now, so why don't you come upstairs and put your work away. Ra'ab's got the kettle on, I think." He rose stiffly, rubbing his back. "I've been sitting too long in the car."

"Right," I said, "I'll put my things away and be up in a few minutes."

Ra'ab was in the kitchen making the tea by the time I had tidied up and climbed the stairs. I went through to tell her about the watch and show her how it looked. "Oh," she greeted me, "Chen's in the bathroom but the tea's almost ready. Did you remember to get the Rich Tea biscuits? I can't find them."

"Goodness, no, I completely forgot. Sorry, can we have something else?"

She looked annoyed. "No, you know he likes Rich Tea. What a nuisance. Anyway, what is it?"

"I just wanted to show you the watch. Look how beautiful it is, Ra'ab." I held out my wrist, but she barely glanced at it.

"It's just an old one, probably won't keep time," she remarked. "You mustn't get the idea that you're special just because he gave you a watch, you know. He's always giving people things. And besides, the truth is you're not special." She reached into the cupboard for cups and saucers, then banged them down on the tray. "And another thing, you're going to have to change the way you talk if you're going to stay with us. No one can understand what you're talking about, you sound as if you think you're superior or something, affected. Yes, that's it, affected." She poured milk into the jug and picked up the tray. "I'm only telling you for your own good. Come along, then, and have some tea. We'll have to do without biscuits, but Chen won't like it."

I followed her into the big room and sat down in my usual place. What a mean old cow! She acted like a deluge of cold water on one's enthusiasms sometimes.

"Ku'ei likes that chair, you know, its really hers. " Ra'ab told me as she passed my tea.

"Yes, I know, but she prefers anyone's lap, especially Chen's." I had no intention of moving until I was ready any more than I was prepared to change the way I talked. "I think I'll go for a walk this evening and perhaps see a picture if there's anything good on," I said. "So I'll skip supper"

"You can't go alone," Chen told me. "It doesn't look good." Strangely, when it concerned me, he was always more worried about appearances than I ever was or could be, but there was no reason to upset him.

"Oh well, I'll just go for a walk then, and early bed." I drank my tea, then rose to leave. "Thank you again so much for the beautiful present. I love it and shall wear it most of the time, and – so far – its ticking away and keeping time. It seems to me that watches have always stopped on me before, no matter what"

"I think you'll find it works all right. Timepieces are very engaging things, you know, personalities in a way." He smiled. "Goodnight, then."

Ra'ab sniffed disdainfully. I was becoming accustomed to her moods. It was easier for me than for Chen which was some consolation.

So far as I recall, it was early autumn, and by the time I left the flat for my walk it was dusk, it would be around six o'clock, I imagine. I can remember London extremely well, although it is years since I last visited that city, but I remember Dublin only sketchily, that is to say the street names escape me, and the distances between different locations. We lived in Nassau Street - I do remember that one - and it could not have been too far from the centre of the city because I remember walking to the Post Office that evening, and I would say the Post Office represented the centre of the city, a large imposing building where reportedly a handful of gallant Irish had held off the British in the times of 'The Troubles.' It has never been forgotten, and probably never will be. The River Liffey flows nearby, and I was standing looking at the bleak, grey, waters, and idly wondering to myself how suicides had the courage to jump to their death, when I heard my name being called. I turned around, startled, and saw an old friend, Julian Chalmers, approaching with long strides from the other side of the street.

"Well, well, it IS you Sheelagh! What on earth are you doing here all alone in the moonlight?" Julian had been my first beau when I was sixteen, and although I seldom ran into him since my marriage, we had one of those firm friendships that do not require constant meetings. I was more than delighted to see him that evening. It turned out that he was on leave, his regiment just having returned from overseas and he was out of touch, as he put it, and had heard nothing about my upheavals. My impression was that he was somewhat appalled when I told him I was virtually on my own, but he was, and had always been, exquisitely courteous and diplomatic. Taking me by the elbow he said, "Now, come along old girl, let's toddle off and get a drink. You look as though you need one. You don't look so chipper, I have to say, although still, of course, your own beautiful self."

Julian clearly was no stranger to Dublin. As we walked along together I remembered him telling about his childhood in Ireland, now I came to think of it, miles away on the West coast somewhere.

"Galway," he said, "My mother's there, father died a few years ago. I'm on my way to see the old sport, spend a few days before going back to London. I inherited the place, of course, so there are things to see to."

"Is it a castle, Julian?"

"A castle? No, I wouldn't say so. Do you like castles or something? It's a big old Georgian pile. Pretty, but takes a hell of a lot to maintain. Why don't you run down there with me? It'd be awfully jolly. It'd do you good."

In no time at all we were cosily ensconced in some smart bar below street level. I had been past the place dozens of times without really noticing the door we entered now, it was so nondescript, just a brown door. Once over the threshold, however, and down a few steps the atmosphere was welcoming and elegant, unlike anything I had been accustomed to in my short time in Dublin. Julian insisted on ordering 'a bottle of bubbly to set you right,' and I offered no resistance. He was a charming companion, relaxed, amusing and attentive, and before long the champagne was doing its work. Someone was playing a piano, gentle swing music, the talk around us was restrained, the lights were low without being too dim, and I began to feel happy and entirely at home. I started to tell him about Chen, and I must have run on and opened up to an alarming degree, but he was, after all, a very old friend and easy to talk to. We had a lot in common, we had grown up with the same values and appreciations. Like John, he was my senior by a number of years. Both of them had been through the war, both had seen front line fighting, but neither spoke about it. It had given them, though, an intangible strength or maturity that the rest of us lacked.

He let me talk on for a while, all the time twirling his moustache and nodding, encouraging my confidence. Then he leant across the table purposefully and said, "You must've 'got religion' or something, you know. I think you should calm down, old girl. It all sounds pretty weird to me."

"Don't be ridiculous, Julian. You know very well I'm opposed to religion, all that fighting and hatred and pretending it's all so saintly. Remember John's mother and the trouble I had with her? Her telling everyone I was a heathen."

"Yes, I know, but this esoteric stuff, well it isn't logical, you know, it's all a load of hocus pocus, nothing scientific about it. You can't prove any of it, it's all just imagination. I'm surprised you let yourself get sucked in. I bet you this fellow you're so full of is a fraud. I'm only telling you for your own good before it's too late. You can still go back to John and patch things up. You shouldn't get involved in all this nonsense." He looked at me earnestly, entirely convinced of the rightness and validity of his opinion.

"Good God, Julian, you're the second person today telling me things for my supposed own good. You simply don't understand, you're a soldier, you have no vision, everything in your world is black or white, no grey areas. But in reality, you know, it's all grey."

"My dear old thing, if it weren't for soldiers you'd be under the Nazis at this very moment. You have to be more balanced, you have to be scientific, you have to use your commonsense and education. Soldiering isn't just a matter of killing the enemy, y'know. You have to work things out, you have to know history, know how the enemy will react, work out strategies, you have to see the world as it really is. You have to know a hell of a lot of things to be a decent soldier! Geography, climate, history, I could go on and on." He leant back, composed and sure of himself. "I think you seriously under-estimate me."

"Well, never mind, Julian. I loathe arguing as you may remember. Let's say no more."

"Very well, but you will come down to visit the mater with me, won't you? Come to that, you could stay with her for a bit, she'd love another woman around the place. You'd like her, quite a character, I'd say, not in the least like old Ma Rouse."

"No, sorry, Julian, I can't." I got up. " It's awfully sweet of you, and it's lovely to see you again. You're a dear to be concerned about me, but I'm perfectly all right, really I am." I kissed him lightly on the cheek. "Don't see me home, I'm off now."

I picked up my handbag. He stood up to stop me, but I was running up the stairs before he really knew what was happening. I remember the look on his face amazement, disappointment, concern. I never saw him again. I doubt he is still alive. Dear old Julian!

* * *

I am not sure exactly how long we stayed in Dublin, but it would be a matter of months rather than years. Chen and Ra'ab had seen a house they liked in Howth, a stone house, square and solid, standing on the cliff edge overlooking a large rock, more like an island although a tiny one, called Ireland's Eye. You had to drive through the village and take the Balscadden Road up the hill towards the Bailey lighthouse, and there was the house, almost the last, or perhaps the very last house before reaching the point. It was for rent, and seemed the ideal place for a us. I liked living there, we all liked living there. Ra'ab had found a second Siamese cat who had been abandoned and we had taken the little thing in. We called her Fifi - Mrs. Fifi Greywhiskers. Both Chen and Ra'ab adored cats. It seems that many of really intelligent people gravitate towards cats, Siamese in particular. They are apparently easy to telepethize with, being of superior intelligence as a breed.

While we lived in Howth, Chen did an astonishing amount of things, he was never idle. He often rowed himself over to Ireland's Eye, and probably sat in silent contemplation there, a perfect setting with only the sound of the wind and the sea, and the crying of the sea birds. He kept a small rowing boat pulled up on the shingle directly below our house. There was a path down the rock, roughly hewn by animals and the odd person, but a path nonetheless. However, he rigged up a rope lashed firmly around a stout tree and invariably slid down the rope to the boat. It was actually easier for him than the path, given his spinal problems and the difficulty of navigating a rough path down a steep rocky slope.

Occasionally he would hire a larger motor boat and get the boatman, Eric, who soon became a friend, to take him out for several hours. Eric had a large family, large even by Irish Catholic standards, living in near poverty, and Chen did a lot to help them, actually paying for one son to be educated by the Christian Brothers. The boy was different from the rest of the family, and the education he received seemed, and no doubt was, his birthright.

Photography was on-going. We continued to have models come out on the bus from Dublin, cars were not a common commodity then for the working people. We still were constantly changing or upgrading equipment, and we bought a small three-wheeled car that looked like a ridiculous bubble bumping along over rough roads. It was called a Heinkel and it could accommodate two people, the driver and one passenger, sitting side by side inside the bubble. It did overtime with trips back and forth to Dublin.

As well as photography, which was essentially work, Chen became passionate about constructing a model railroad, an ambitious and fascinating hobby with tracks all around his room and beyond, sophisticated and realistic, and the Dublin trips were a necessity for a time to choose and purchase the almost daily additions of track, engines, freight cars, passenger carriages, signals, buildings, towns, mountains, trees, animals, people, a mininature world in fact. We would have two or three trains running at a time, the trick being to keep them all on their respective tracks and to stop the cats from derailing them.

On the way to Dublin we would often drive on a sandy stretch of beach, Clontarf it was called, and as frequently got into trouble with quick sands. Mercifully and amazingly, we never completely lost the car, although we came near once or twice! Chen had a boyish, daredevil streak which made life amusing and nerve-wracking by turn. I have distinct memories of seeing the minute vehicle visibly sinking while we struggled with shovels, or am I dreaming? Life was never dull.

It must have been on the sands at Clontarf, this one particular day that comes to mind. We were photographing model ships that day, something we did for a time, making them realistic on film by arranging small rocks, placing the models in pools of water simulating the ocean, everything to size. We must have been resting. I can see in my mind's eye a far off image of Chen idly scooping up a handful of sand and letting it trickle through his hand. He had started to call me Buttercup. It amused him to give nicknames, and I was to have several during the years we lived together.

"See these tiny grains of sand, Buttercup? Our lives are no more than that, no more significant or important when seen in the real scale of things, and a life is over in the wink of an eye. But - without each tiny insignificant grain of sand there would be no beach." He dipped his hand in the pool, and let the water run through, drop by drop. "When you come to the end of life you'll see it as it is, as no more than a drop in the ocean. When you come to the end you'll see before you in a flash all your life. Perhaps we could call that hell, because we are seldom proud of what we see. We are hard judges, you know, when it comes to judging ourselves, and we do judge ourselves, we are not judged by a God, as some religions teach. There is no God waiting for you like a benevolent or strict old gentleman, no host of angels, unless it is delusionary because your religious belief demands such a delusion for a time after death until you are ready for truth. Your own Overself is your God, the one to whom you pray, and you return to that entity – to your Higher Self or Overself – at death, taking back the experience you have gained while living on Earth. You leave your physical body behind just like an old suit of clothes. It served your purpose for that particular life, you have no more need of it."

He sighed, and paused before continuing. "I maintain that life on earth is too hard, it's so hard that it often teaches nothing. Do you realise that a huge proportion of humanity exists in appalling conditions, they long for death, how can they understand that it all has a purpose?" He fell silent, gazing into the distance. I was aware of a surge of concern and empathy emanating from him, but not hopelessness. For him there was always hope.

I said nothing. The small boat we had been photographing bobbed and turned in the shallow pool, and I watched it as I tried to assimilate what he had just said. I recall that it was hard then to understand concepts which now are completely obvious. When you can look back and remember, it is only then that you grasp the reason for a long life, the time given to you to progress and find your own truth. Some may reach that point sooner than others, but it seems there is always a little more just beyond one's comprehension. It brings to mind lines by the Argentian poet, Alejandra Pizarnik:

'And if the soul were to ask, How much further?

You must answer: On the other side of the river,

Not this one, the one just beyond.'

"There's a basic flaw, you know, with humans," Chen went on. "For millions and millions of years different species have been on this planet. Now the human is in control but things aren't going well, humans are headed for self-destruction. It's a matter of concern for the entire universe."

"A flaw? What, then, is the basic flaw that we have?" I asked.

"It isn't known precisely. When you are part of a thing you can't see it, it becomes normal because everyone is affected to a greater or lesser degree, and those in the astral are too remote from the physical to be able to diagnose and correct it. People like me are trying to understand it. We have to have good and we have to have bad to maintain balance, I've told you that often, but the bad seems to have gone rampant, the negative is far, far stronger than the positive, like a garden strangled by weeds."

"Can't people be warned? There are lots of good people."

"Warn them!! Ah, Buttercup, if you only knew! I've warned individuals in the past when they've sought my opinion, and almost without exception (I have to say you are the exception that proves the rule) they have become angry, and blamed ME for somehow putting the evil eye on them. No, it doesn't work to warn people because they lack faith, and certainly one can't warn world leaders - the big powers don't want to know to begin with. They are obsessed with power and greed. By the end of the century there will be fireworks in the Middle East, terrible trouble.

"I'm not the only one who knows that, but how to stop it – I don't know – it's almost at the point of no return."

We sat for a while, silent, both with our own thoughts. I remember feeling overcome with the enormity of what he was telling me. I did not think then that I would be alive at the turn of the century, but here I am, and what he predicted has come to pass. What he predicted about gains in knowledge and acceptance of esoteric and mystical concepts is also happening.

A thing is only mystical until it is understood by science. Although I personally profess to be a Luddite (those 19th century artisans who objected to machinery and were accused of obstructing progress), and view modern advanced technology as a step away from spiritual development, Chen insisted that advanced technology would be responsible for general awareness of things that psychic people are already aware of. Because of that, he was always intensely interested in technological advances.

The day was lengthening and clouds were gathering. "I think it's time we were getting home," he remarked, getting stiffly to his feet. I stowed the cameras, light meter and tripod into the tiny vehicle, while he took the boats from the water and carefully stood them up side by side in a cardboard box so no damage would occur on the return journey. A lot of work had gone into their construction. He usually took the wheel and I sat beside him. He had a way with machines, loving to tinker, whether it be cars, boats, aeroplanes, motor bikes, even typewriters responding to his touch and seeming to perform better after his going over them.

That night lying in bed I began to realize the unique position I, by some kind of fluke, occupied. I was well aware of the great number of others who envied or were jealous of my closeness to one whom they regarded as a Master. If I thought about it seriously, I would have had to admit that I had no qualifications, no special knowledge, although I did earnestly and sincerely wish to understand what life was all about. It had plagued and puzzled me since I was a child and I had agonized over the whole question until I met Chen, and then, almost as soon as I met him, I had realized he possessed the answers I sought. Sleep was never long in coming in those days, the bracing sea air and emotional tranquility of life guaranteed a deep dreamless sleep, and I dropped off easily, satisfied with what life had to offer and my place in it.

It would be around that time that a man named Naughton crossed our path again. He had appeared briefly in London, arriving on our doorstep one day unannounced, uninvited and, I have to say, unwelcome. But his blue eyes and naive manner coupled with a winning smile gained him entry, how could one send him away? He seemed charm and innocence personified. As well, he was greatly enthused by 'The Third Eye,' and being of an aristocratic background it simply never occurred to him that he would not be immediately admitted to our menage. It quickly became apparent that he felt he and Chen would benefit mutually from the contact, and such was indeed the case. His work was in the field of a diagnostic device with a group in the south of England, not yet accepted by the medical or scientific fraternities, nor completely understood by its users, and he felt that Chen would be able to clarify and assist in its use. Naughton himself, as it turned out, was a qualified medical doctor, but with an interest in matters beyond the range of current scientific discovery - futuristic would be a good way to describe him.

When we moved to Ireland he seemed to fade out of sight, partly because he obtained a job as ship's doctor on a luxury liner, while still intending to return to his research work, and also because we left London during his time overseas. It was a surprise, then, when we received a letter from him saying he was back in England and would be able to come to visit. Did we realize, the letter went on, that Ireland was his real homeland, he knew Dublin well although he seldom returned there these days.

In his customary manner he arrived unheralded close on the heels of the letter, a small, slight man, bearded and wearing a belted navy blue raincoat, his hands thrust deep into the pockets, with no invitation and to Chen's undisguised displeasure. Unabashed, he seated himself beside Chen's bed as though he belonged there. He was possessive, singular. Naughton had been born a woman, and the complicated process of changing his sex had been completed only quite recently. I was never told, and in any case was not especially interested in knowing, what his birth name was, but he would have been hard pressed to have chosen a more masculine name for himself after the gender change, and, to tell the truth, it was a poor choice. It simply did not suiit him. He would never be a masculine man. He must have experienced great emotional upheavals as well as physical changes, and he still possessed, and undoubtedly always would, those characteristics commonly associated with women. He had small expressive hands, fine bones, and strong feelings. Within he must surely have been in turmoil, although he strove to hide it. He had no great love for me mainly because he envied my closeness to Chen, and whenever I was alone with him he could barely be civil. I kept my distance.

I feel sure it was during that visit that the full significance of my relationship with Chen came home to me. We had known each other for perhaps a couple of years by this time, maybe more, and his transition from an anonymous life of struggle to one of being famous throughout the world had come upon him so quickly that I had not truly acknowledged it to myself. To me he had simply written a book to enable him to get on with his true purpose, his real work. That was how I saw it. I had always known he was a Master, but looking back, my attitude seems remarkably unrealistic. Perhaps I was living in a land of make- believe where things were as I wanted them to be, not as they actually were. Had I not been dealing with scores of letters from people all over the world, anxious to get a glimpse of him? Had I not seen his book prominently displayed? Of course I had, and it was time to admit that he was famous, it was time to admit that he was seen as a wonder and a saviour to millions of spiritually starved people everywhere. The fact that he remained as private as possible, refusing to see people or give lectures, the fact that he ignored or shunned cults which were springing up and which used his knowledge as their teaching, made the pursuit of him even greater. But fame is a weighty companion to most, and to Chen it was distasteful in the extreme.

Howth was a pretty place, there were beautiful walks along the coast on the cliffs, and habitually I took a walk each evening and sometimes early in the morning, when only the wild creatures, the soaring seagulls and the crash of the waves were my companions. Usually there was a sea mist and a heavy dew on the ground, so I kept close to the cliffs, where the grass was sparse and it was drier for walking. This particular day I have in mind was no different from any other except that I suddenly became aware of dislodged stones behind me, and a startled pee-wit taking to wing, uttering his cry as he skimmed past. I turned, surprised.

"Why, Naughton, I didn't know you liked an early walk."

"I don't, but I know you do." He straightened himself from his stumble, brushing off his trousers. "I've been following you, you know." As he said it, he smiled, not his charming, disarming smile, but a smile with a threat behind it, an evil smile, his eyes narrowing. "It would be so easy to push you over, no one would ever know, they'd think you'd missed your footing."

"Well, indeed, what a charming thought, Naughton! Only you would be capable of such a thoroughly unpleasant idea." I smiled back at him, equally mirthlessly. "Why would anyone want to push me over?"

"Why? I'll tell you. Because you're just a damned nuisance, a hindrance to Chen and his work. He needs a man beside him, someone intelligent. You can't even play chess!" My chess playing was an issue with Naughton, I did not take it seriously enough. It infuriated him – as many things did. He was, in truth, an old maid, no matter how much one tried to excuse him.

"Well, I think you're being a fool." I moved away from the cliff edge. He was someone you could never be sure of, he was unbalanced emotionally and he might be absolutely serious in his plan to get rid of me. "I'm going home now and I don't especially want to walk home with you." I set off at a fast pace. I was used to walking, and knew I could outstrip him, even if he started to run. But he made no attempt to keep up with me. It was as if he had missed a golden opportunity and knew himself defeated.

I never mentioned that incident to anyone, but I remembered it and learned from it. Chen unleashed strong emotions in people, and it was best for me to stay away from anyone he was taking under his wing temporarily, as he frequently did. He actually encouraged my stance, as though he knew – and, of course, he did – the dangers, the jealousies and unpleasantness that could ensue.

CHAPTER SIX

It may have been Lady Shane and her black Raleigh bicycle with the red stripe that inspired me to get one of my own. The sight of her bowling along in all weathers, so healthy and so free, was quite splendid. She never had to wait for a bus, buy petrol, or fuss about repairs to a car. She simply took off when the spirit moved her.

It seemed, therefore, whichever way you looked at it, a good idea to get a bicycle, and I had been toying with the idea for a few weeks when, quite by chance, I came across one which was for sale in the village. I reasoned that it would save time, I could sail down the hill to the little kiosk by the bus stop each morning to collect the newspaper in no time at all. I could cycle into the village and bring home groceries in the nice ample basket resting on the handlebars. There was even a carrier on the back for transporting all kinds of flat things. I could pedal down to the dock and along the quay in the evenings to buy freshly caught fish from the fishing boats as they moored up alongside and unloaded their catch. I might even cycle into Dublin. So, even though it was nowhere near the equal of the Shane bicycle, I purchased it, and very quickly felt confident and completely roadworthy.

For a while the bicycle played a large part in my life. Freewheeling down hills with the wind in one's face was exhilarating. Cycling past people with a jolly wave instead of being expected to stop and chat about nothing in particular, as one would on foot, was gratifying. The downside was that hills go both ways, up and down, and the ascending part, pushing the thing, was not only tedious, it was hard work. My machine was not equipped with several gears to make things easier, nothing of that sort, it was just a plain workaday affair. But, for all that, the bicycle offered an appealing kind of independence. My legs could and did take me places, but now I had a vehicle of sorts that actually mobilised one very effectively, and although the travel was anything but fast, it gave the illusion of speed – especially the downhills!

I still walked along the cliffs early in the morning, but after breakfast I would get out the bicycle, and speed off down the hill, round the bend, down another hill to the bus stop on the front, right beside the shop. It was a kind of gathering place, this kiosk-type shop, the hub of the village where anyone coming or going from Dublin had to either alight or depart, anyone, that is, except the elite who went by car – or bicycle – and there were not many of those. In the summer there were tourists – visitors might be a better word for them, tourism not having reached today's dizzy heights – dallying around, killing time, breathing in the fresh salt air, and marvelling at the beauty of the place. In the winter there were locals picking up their newspaper, buying a loaf of bread, a packet of cigarettes, or simply just out for a morning stroll and a gossip. I knew them all, some better than others. The neat, plump woman behind the counter would hand me the newspaper, tucking in stray strands of hair, or smoothing her apron with the other hand as she enquired did we want anything else, a bit of sugar, milk, perhaps? Behind her, arrayed on the shelves, were packets of tea, biscuits, bars of chocolate, radio batteries, toothpaste, aspirins and the odd cheap paperback novel or local road map rubbing shoulders with bottles of pop and boxes of matches. There were bottles of evil looking liquid for coughs, tins of baked beans and corned beef. If you looked long enough you found what it was you wanted in that tiny place.

Chen was experiencing a recurrence of heart trouble. It had started before we left London, coronary thrombosis, but seemed reasonably under control after we left the hustle and bustle of a big city. He had a local doctor visit the house from time to time, "Just in case I don't manage to keep going," he would say. "If I'm known to be ill there'll be no trouble with the death certificate." Dr. B. was a pleasant, kindly man and, once he mastered his hesitation about visiting a heathen home and found us civilized enough, was comfortable in his role as physician. He lived in Sutton Cross, a small place on the road to Dublin, and was easy to access if we needed him.

This particular morning which was to change our lives immeasurably, Chen was still sleeping when I left the house, cranked open the garage door and wheeled the bicycle out, taking care not to bump the Heinkel as I went. After shutting the door I glanced at the hotel on the opposite side of the bay, appropriately named The Cliff Hotel, as it seemed to hang on the cliff in a similar manner to our house. Although with binoculars it was possible to see into the windows, and equally possible for them to see into ours, one supposed, it was never of interest to us in any way. This morning, however, there were people around at the windows. I could see them moving, not distinctly, the distance was too great, but as black shadows. It was unusual, but I did not even stop to wonder who or what they were. I was off down the hill, elated and happy. It was a nippy morning, the brisk chill wind was holding the rain off, it cleared one's head and got the day going to a good start. As I rounded the final bend, and was freewheeling down towards the kiosk I was struck by the aura of agitation surrounding a little knot of people close beside the shop. Something had happened, something momentous by the look of it. There must have been eight or nine people, all with newspapers in their hand. What could it be, I wondered. Maybe the Queen had died, maybe someone had been murdered in a particularly gruesome manner. It would have to be something quite dreadful to create such a ripple in the normal placid demeanour of these people whom I met each day, and who greeted me so affably each morning, never unduly excited about anything, the weather being our main topic.

I alighted from my bicycle and wheeled it towards the shop, as I always did. The group melted away at my approach, no one looking directly at me. How odd, it must be something terribly English that was upsetting them, and knowing my nationality they were embarrassed, the Irish were like that, highly conscious of nationality. Maybe some awful bill had been passed in the House of Lords demeaning the Irish and I was getting the blame for it.

"Good morning, Mrs. O'Rourke," I greeted the proprietess of the shop, smiling at her.

"Oh, good morning, miss." her voice was thin with emotion of some sort, and higher than usual. She was behaving like an amateur actress on the stage for the first time, self-conscious, not knowing where to place her hands, not able to meet my eyes. Her nervousness was unsettling. What on earth was this all about, I asked myself. After handing me the newspaper, she scuttled off through the door at the back of the shop, mumbling about getting the kettle on for breakfast. No friendly invitation to buy tea, no enquiries about the 'good doctor.' This morning it was different, and oddly confusing.

Leaning against the bicycle to prop it up, I opened the newspaper – and nearly dropped it. So that was it! I was met by a half page photograph of myself, taken years ago by Pearl Freeman, a society photographer, on my engagement to John for inclusion in 'The Tatler.' It was still, so many years later, recognizable. The caption, however, was the disturbing part: 'Society Hostess Flees with Bogus Lama,' it read in large, black print.

Momentarily knocked out of myself by shock, deliberately and carefully I folded the newspaper and secured it on the back of the bicycle. I found myself unfocussed, weak and unsteady on my legs, adrenalin was flowing. Hardly knowing what I was doing, I wheeled past the group of people, yesterday's friends, their backs now turned towards me. Understandably, perhaps, they had no wish to meet my gaze, neither did I wish to encounter their's. I crossed the road safely, and reaching a bench beside the quay sat down on it, letting the bicycle crash to the ground, unheeded. After a minute or two I took the newspaper out from under the carrier and skimmed it. I had to know what was in it before I took it home. Chen was in a delicate state of health, and it looked as though there was some appalling lying scandal brewing. He had to be protected. It would be devastating for him. Even good publicity was abhorrent to him. He was essentially a hermit, and to be foisted into the public eye in such a manner as this would be agony for him, it could even prove fatal.

Opening the newspaper again, my first thought was of outrage that I could be described as a 'society hostess.' It conjured up the image of a hard, brittle, wealthy and thoroughly unpleasant woman, far from the way I could ever see myself, or had ever been. But that was only the beginning. This allusion to myself was merely in the trumped up story to make Chen out to be the worst kind of lecher possible, and to pander to scandal mongers. The story inside the newspaper was lengthy, and I was unable to bring myself to read it in full. I got the gist, though - it was insulting, hurtful, and untrue. I could not imagine what had occurred, who would make up such things and why, but one thing I knew – it had to be stopped. With my resolve clear, I mounted the bicycle and set off for home, not caring about anything now except to see justice done, to protect Chen. I pedalled furiously as far up the hill as my legs and lungs permitted, then dismounted and pushed with vigour and a newfound energy. Rounding the last bend before the house, a fresh horror was waiting, what seemed like a throng of people, men crowded around the steps leading to the front door, and Ra'ab standing on the top step outside the door, looking fearful and agitated. Then it dawned on me. The press! My God, it was the press, all those people at the Cliff Hotel, that was what it was, the press waiting to pounce. But why so many?

Ra'ab saw me first, and tried to signal for me to keep away. They followed her motions, and turning saw me approaching. In an instant I was surrounded, microphones were thrust at me, cameras were clicking, they were shouting at me, asking questions. In a sudden rage I grabbed the newspaper and rolled it into a hard tight stick. Holding it over my head, I thrashed at them furiously telling them to leave us alone, to get out of our way. Such unexpected anger and threatening demeanour had some effect, and I was able to reach Ra'ab unmolested. I pushed her inside the house and slammed the door, locking it, and leaned my back against it.

"You shouldn't have done that, you shouldn't have done it, upset them," Ra'ab whispered urgently, as if they could hear through the closed door. "They're from all over the world, and they can print terrible things about us if you upset them." Normally she was rather flat in her manner when not over-elated, and to see her in such a state of vulnerability was surprising. She seemed afraid and awed, in contrast to my own reaction. But then, she had not seen the newspaper yet.

"They've already said terrible things about us, terrible lies," I told her. "You haven't seen the newspaper. It's got to be stopped. I'm going to London - now, right away. If I hurry I can catch the morning plane." I was already half way downstairs to my room on the lower level of the house. I could telephone Ed Finnigan, the local taxi driver, to pick me up further up the hill. I could take the cliffside path and meet him beyond our house, so no one would see me going. I had it planned. But I had to hurry.

Ra'ab followed me to the top of the stairs. "What will Chen say when he knows you're gone. He'd never let you go. If he weren't so ill I'd tell him and he'd stop you. You're so headstrong, he's the only one can manage you." She was almost wailing, but I had no time to feel sorry for her. I had to get to London and see a solicitor immediately.

"I can't help that, I'm going!" I had about ten minutes to change my clothes, fix my face and make sure I had English money in my purse. My mind was working rapidly, and I knew I could do it.

We often went out to the airport to watch planes landing and departing. It was a pleasant run, the road winding through pretty, gentle country and passing the only turf cottage I remember ever seeing. Dublin was a small airport in those days, too small for large aircraft, Shannon in the south west of Eire being the international airport. But this day I scarcely noticed the route or the time we took, my mind was racing ahead of me. Ed was our friend, and I sat beside him. He was silent and tactful, only once as we were nearing the airport turning to me as he scratched his head, "I'm that sorry, miss, 'tis a shame indeed. The poor doctor, himself such a gentleman. Lyin' bastards, that's what they are those English papers, lyin' bastards."

"Yes, I know, thank you, Ed. I expect to be back on the last plane. Do you think you can meet me?"

"Indeed I can, miss. God be wid ye," were his parting words as I opened the car door.

I could see the plane standing ready to leave, there was no time to waste if I was to catch it. I ran inside to buy my ticket, then sprinted across the tarmac, thankfully taking a seat at the back of the plane just in time for takeoff. Aer Lingus was a small, friendly airline, and the smart young hostess was calming and pleasant. The minute we were airborne I felt better, resolving problems, excited almost. I was young and optimistic. During the short flight, I had time to collect myself a little and decide exactly how to handle the plan I had embarked upon, perhaps a little recklessly, it now seemed.

Brian Carruthers had been a close friend of John's since schooldays, one of the few with whom he kept in close contact, and now had become a friend of us both. A clever QC, I felt sure he could help me, advise me what to do, how to stop the newspapers, how to sue them if necessary. He was the person who first occurred to me, and he was the person I was determined to see. He might be in court, of course, he might be away in Europe or who-knows-where else. He might not be able to see me at all, and I supposed I should have rung him up before undertaking this trip – but then, I had no time to spare, I reasoned. I ruminated on all this as coffee was served and cleared away. My plan was that when we landed I would take the airport bus to Earl's Court, and from there a taxi to Lincoln's Inn. Brian's chambers were in the Inner Temple. I reasoned that to telephone from Earl's Court or even from the airport saying I was coming would not be a good idea, I might be told in no uncertain terms that there was no chance of seeing him. Instead, I would simply arrive as though he was expecting me, and with luck I would be shown in. The chances were that luck would be with me. And, as it turned out, so it was – up to a point.

"My dear Sheelagh, lovely to see you!" Brian seemed almost to have been waiting for me, or was it my imagination? He kissed me with seeming affection, and signalled for me to take the large armchair across from his own.

The place was luxurious, impressive, oak panelling, thick carpeting, silent, hundreds of books carefully arranged in expensive bookcases, silver framed photographs. I had never seen him in chambers previously, and I remember finding it all a little daunting. My own life had become so simple in the few months I had been away from London, this was in complete contrast.

"I'm so sorry about the nonsense in the morning papers.," he said as I settled myself. "Muckrakers, they are, just pandering to the Great Unwashed. A bad affair, a bad affair. But now, what can I do for you?" He offered a cigarette as he spoke.

Brian listened gravely as I explained my situation, my concern for Chen. When I had finished he seemed to be locked in thought. He said nothing, remained silently smoking, giving the impression that he was considering my case, but for all I knew he may have been thinking about something entirely different, perhaps his current big case, he may have made up his mind about me even before I arrived. Then, after a long pause, and to my considerable surprise he said, "The best thing you can do, you know, is to leave these people, just don't go back. They won't do you any good, its a nasty scandal, not the kind of thing you want to be mixed up in. We all do stupid things, I suppose, and you have, if you will forgive my saying so, behaved somewhat oddly. Girls like you just don't walk out of marriages openly to live in squalor, it isn't done. You could very well find you're not accepted, you could be snubbed by people you've been brought up with, people who have the same code of behaviour. But never mind, you'll live it down, in a year or two no one will remember anything about it."

He stubbed out his cigarette, fixing me with an almost hypnotic stare. It would have been no surprise if a wig had appeared on his head and a gown over his shoulders. "You simply can't get mixed up in this sordid business, you really can't," he repeated emphatically. " If you persist, then not only will you become persona non grata with your own kind, you'll find you're not accepted or understood by 'them,' by the other kind of people. You'll fall between two stools. Think about your future."

I was amazed. I had not asked his opinion on such matters.

Then he went on,, "As for the newspapers – there's not a thing anyone can do to stop them printing this stuff. It's what they've been told. It's probably true, anyway."

So there was my answer. He believed the newspaper story, he believed that Chen was a fake, he believed all the scandalous things said about him. He believed it - but I, on the other hand, I knew it was made up, I knew it was lies. I knew Chen. That was the difference between us. I was deflated. There was no point in telling him anything to try to change his opinion. It was almost as if he had been briefed, almost as if it was expected I would go to him for advice, but the thing was, I was seeking a different kind of advice from that expected. Then, as he obviously had no more to say, and was behaving like some superior schoolmaster with a recalcitrant child, I got up with what dignity I could muster. "I see, Brian," I said, " Good of you to see me at such short notice and take the time to give your advice." Part of me truly wished I could thank him and tell him I would do as he suggested. Part of me regretted having to turn aside from well-meaning friends. I walked towards the door.

As if he knew what I was thinking he said, "If you are unable or unwilling to heed my advice, you'll regret it, Sheelalgh."

I remember standing outside on the pavement wondering what to do next. "Girls like you," he had said. That was the problem, or part of it. I was not one of 'those girls.' I was beginning to feel hungry and jittery. My plan had fallen flat. Perhaps some food would help, would restore some sort of order to my mind. Although I love London, I found the crowds and the noise distressful. Howth was so quiet and peaceful. My club was in Charles Street, just off Berkeley Square, and I decided to head that way, get some lunch and ring up John from there. I could take a bus, that would be a nice stabilizing thing to do, then I could walk from Piccadilly down Berkeley Street. It was not too far and the day was clear.

I sat on the top deck at the back when the bus came. As we crawled through the London traffic, stopping and starting in that familiar jolting way London buses have, I felt a strange kind of sadness come over me. Brian had tried to help, he had gone out of his way to ensure I would do what he personally believed was the correct thing, he had invited me back into the fold despite my transgression, my breaking the rules and stepping out of line. I wished I could thank him, explain to him that I was not like that, not one of 'those girls.' I would tell John, and perhaps one day it would get back to him, although it was out of the question to imagine that he might understand. He would just shrug and write the whole thing off as being beyond him.

Unlike Cordelia who belonged to the Lansdowne, my club was far from being the smartest in London, but it was safe and always had been even when I was a teenager far from home who needed a club from time to time. The members, for the most part, were elderly, dowdy, and respectable, but the fees were reasonable, the dining room presentable and it was somewhere to go where no one would be interested in me or in the scandalous newspapers. As I toyed with lunch my mind went to Chen and Ra'ab. She had been right, of course, I had been a fool to think that I could single-handedly stop the press, a fool to rush off like that, and maybe Chen was wondering if I had taken off because of the trouble. I must get back, stop him worrying, especially in his present state of health. But I had missed the afternoon plane by this time, and would have to wait until late for the next and last one of the day. In any case, I was anxious to talk to John. When I got through to him, perched on a worn velvet seat in the telephone booth in the hall of the club, he seemed not at all surprised to hear my voice. "Your parents are at Brown's, they'd like to see you, " he said.

"At Brown's? What are they doing in town? Why do they want to see me? You know I can't see them. We'll just go through all the recriminations over and over, uselessly."

"Mm, I suppose so," he was his typical self, keeping out of it, trying to placate me. "All the same, you really should see them in view of this business. I'll come with you if you like." His voice over the telephone gave little away. But that was John, always cautious, always sitting on the fence. So I agreed. He would pick me up at the club and we would go together.

Brown's Hotel was a smallish, rather quiet and exclusive place in those days, and perhaps still is. We found my parents installed in a corner of the lounge, sitting in front of a large Chinese screen. It was a shock to see them, they seemed like strangers. My father, always courteous and gentle, was really no different, I had just forgotten how he was. Tall and good looking, he had his usual cigarette in his hand and a drink nearby. My mother was sitting as if enthroned. She did not know what had happened to this daughter she had so carefully moulded. Something had gone wrong. Her favourite adage – 'Give me a child 'til he's seven and he's mine for life' – had somehow failed her. Things had to be put back in their place, her daughter had to be made to come to heel. She was a determined woman who hated to be thwarted, because she knew she was right. She was wearing a delightful, sexy pink hat, but it was at odds with her manner and expression. Her mink stole was draped around her shoulders, and if the little dead mouths had opened to bite and snarl it would have been more in keeping with their wearer. She was small and dark, my mother, but upright and threatening. I felt glad that John was with me. They liked him.

My father rose, smiling. My mother remained seated. "So you've returned, have you?" was her greeting. "After making a laughing stock of us all and pulling us through the mud, you come crawling back now you've found out about your fine friend."

"Returned? No, I haven't. You wanted to see me?" I was surprisingly calm and detached.

What happened next was almost surreal. As if summoned by the devil, a little man suddenly appeared in our midst. Had he come from a hole in the floor, or had he dropped from the sky? Neither, he had emerged from behind the screen, like a character in a comedy.

"Mrs. Rouse, allow me to introduce myself – Jeremiah Smythe, private detective."

Ignoring his attempt to shake hands with me, I remained standing, watching him. Jeremiah Smythe! No one was called Jeremiah Smythe outside Dickens. It must be a nightmare, in a moment I would waken up. But no, he continued:

"Ah, I see you haven't heard of me. Well, let me tell you, my dear young lady, I have spent months tracking down your friend, and he isn't what he says he is, he's been fooling you." He paused. No one said a word.. "So you don't want to know about him, eh? Well, do you know what he is?" Another pregnant pause. " He's a plumber! A common plumber!! An English plumber who has never been outside this country. What do think of that? I have proof, yes, I have proof. He's fooled you, he's fooled everyone, but now the game is up. My proof is here, pages of it." He slapped a large brief case he had placed beside him on the floor.

The pause was longer this time, they were all waiting to see how I would take it. But, poor dears, they were unprepared for what happened next. I felt like Julian, I felt like a good soldier who knows the enemy, who has a strategy to outdo them. Surprise attack. Take them unawares. So I did, I slapped that detestable little man on the cheek not once, but twice. Then I left. Regrettably, I was not there to witness the commotion, to hear and see the sky falling, I was already on the way to the airport, on my way home, the only home I had now. I had well and truly burned my bridges, and Brown's Hotel must have suffered an unheard of broadside that day.

It was not until later that we became aware of the reason behind the scandal that hit Chen so badly and gave rise to so much controversy regarding his identity, controversy that still rages to this day. I am not sure if the detective was hired by my parents or by the German writer who regarded Tibet as his domain and was incensed that Lobsang Rampa had written a book about Tibet that, in his opinion, had popularised the country. This man was one of the few people who had spent time in Tibet, a country at that period quite inaccessible to outsiders. During the war he had taken refuge there (later it was discovered he was a Nazi) but he had never been able to penetrate the inner life of the lamaseries. He may have been jealous or he may have been moved by a mistaken but genuine desire to keep the lamastic life sacred. In any event, he never had the common sense to make direct contact with Chen.

Was it he or who was it? Who was responsible for the publicity and lies that circulated? It was never clear to me. Whoever it was did a grave disservice, and it would not be going too far to say a grave disservice to mankind. Chen sustained an inner injury that I believe never truly healed. Although he continued his work it was always with a struggle which blunted the impact his books and knowledge may otherwise have had.

The fact is, however, that Lobsang Rampa's true identity is not important. WHO Lobsang Rampa was is not the consequential issue, the message he imparted is. But to say he was an English plumber – plumbers then being regarded as illiterates – or an Englishman of any kind who had never been out of his country is so ridiculous as to be ludicrous. Even to the millions who had never met him but had read his books, it should be clearly impossible. I was in the unique position of knowing that his books were entirely spontaneous; there was never any research, never any hesitation or back tracking to correct statements he made, the drawings, even, were basically his, and the map of Lhasa, all done freehand with no references of any kind. He was writing of his own experiences, there is no other possible explanation, and he was using his own knowledge.

True to his word Ed Finnigan was waiting for me at the airport and it was hugely comforting to see his kind, cheery face. By the time we drew up outside the little stone house on the cliff it was very late, and the house appeared to be in darkness. At least, thankfully, there were no signs of dastardly reporters skulking around. I fitted my key to the lock and pushed open the heavy wooden door.

Everything was still, and for a moment I wondered if it had all been too much and Chen had not survived the onslaught that was in progress when I left that same morning. I wondered if he had actually departed this life and was free at last. As I stood there in the semi-darkness I felt a furry body rubbing against my legs, and knew that Ku'ei was greeting me. Chen's room was at the end of the hallway, and an encouraging faint light glowed from the partly opened door. I tiptoed along the hallway and pushed open the door. There before me was Dr. B. kneeling at the rough wooden work table, his head in his hands, oblivious to my entry. I assumed he was praying.

It was a large room, full of Chen's hobbies, studies and scientific belongings. It had a lovely bay window, and his bed was placed there, in the window, looking directly out over the ocean, over the wide expanse of sea and sky with nothing to impede the majesty of the elements. The only sounds were the crash of the waves against the rocks below at high tide, the cry of the sea birds, the changing patterns of the wind, in stormy weather howling and moaning, and the mournful wail of the lighthouse on the point above.

It was a marvellous, invigorating, inspiring spot, and it was tragic that it had been invaded that day by pressmen, so insensitive, so lacking in refinement.

Now, as I stood on the threshold of the room, I saw that the faint light was coming from a lamp placed near the bed. Ra'ab was sitting there with a book in her hands, but the light was so dim it is doubtful she was reading, more likely she was immersed in thought and sorrow. She had many difficulties to contend with in life and, although on a worldy level we often did not meet amicably, I felt great empathy and respect for her and her role at that moment

My eye travelled to the bed where Chen was lying quite still, his profile silhouetted against the blue-black of the night sky, a limpid sky full of stars and a half moon, a sky so pure the like of which one would never see in a city. It formed a magical backdrop. The room smelled of incense.

As I stood waiting, he spoke, "Miss Ku'ei tells me Sheelagh has returned." His voice was thin and lacked life force. The little cat had jumped on the bed and I could just make out her body lying by his side. At least he was alive.

Ra'ab turned and saw me, "Yes, she's returned," she said.

I crossed the room and as I did so the doctor looked up and, crossing himself, rose to his feet. He was leaving. His patient was in the hands of God now. He could do no more. Let the Almighty do what He would.

I knelt beside the bed and took Chen's hand in my own. Now, close to him, it became apparent that his face was deathly pale, his skin moist and clammy.

"I'm glad you came back Buttercup," he said.

"Did you think I wouldn't?"

"One never knows." He remained still and silent for a few minutes, then he said, "I need you to help me. I need energy. Lie close beside me."

I lay on the bed with my body close to his, pressed to his body. I knew I possessed a basic vibration which was harmonious with his own, I knew I had the life force that he so lacked at that moment, I knew I could make him live, I happened to have what he needed. I realised that evening that I was necessary, that he would not continue if I left his side. So I remained by his side for more than twenty years, literally never leaving him for one day or night. "But you won't be there when I die, you know," he told me once, to which I replied, "Don't be ridiculous, I shall always be with you as long as you live." However, he was right in the end. When I finally left he lived for only a few weeks. But I am running on ahead of myself and ahead of my magic painting. Much water flowed under the bridge before we arrived at the parting of the ways.

That night, then, I slowly felt his energy returning. I cannot explain how I felt it. As I have stated before, we have no words in our concrete language to explain esoteric happenings, one just knows. I cannot say how much time elapsed before he said, "You must go to bed now. You're tired. Thank you, Buttercup. I shall be all right now. Goodnight. Ra'ab must go to bed, too. She's had a hard day. She's done well. I shall be all right," he repeated. We knew he would get more help from others in the astral if we left him, not the same kind of crude physical energy I could give him, but assistance of a different order, beyond our understanding.

As I lay in bed I watched the log burning on the hearth, I watched the flickering light and the occasional spit of flame, the glow and comfort of the smouldering wood. The house was damp and we needed fires in rooms we lived and slept in, that was the only heat we had and it was the best kind. Somehow it encouraged deep thought and contemplation. I thought of the superficial lives of people I had seen that day. They were actors on a stage, as are we all, but they were perhaps not conscious of it in the same way I was, they perhaps attached greater importance to things of the flesh than I now did. I knew I had made a silent commitment to Chen, and I knew he knew it. My life henceforth would be withdrawn from society, it would be enriched, though, beyond measure. I knew that by making that commitment it had solidified Chen's resolve to see his job through, to find out the reason for human behaviour, to find the flaw. He needed only one person to commit to him totally to make it worth his while, to make his suffering worth it. I happened to be that person, that average human he needed.

Dr. B., when he came the next morning, was nonplussed. It was not that God never answered his prayers, sometimes He did, there was no denying that. Why only last week old Mrs. O'Grady had rallied, hadn't she? But he had never seen such a sudden and startling turn around as this. It fleetingly crossed his mind that it could be the work of the devil, and as hurriedly he rejected the thought. It wasn't safe to dwell on such things, you never knew what road it could lead you along, especially when you were dealing with heathens. All the same, it was rather like a miracle, whoever had wrought it. He left the house, relieved it had turned out like this, promising to return if there was any change for the worse.

Chen, it is true, was almost restored to his normal appearance although he had a weariness about him which was unaccustomed. The three of us met by his bedside, and I was filled in about the happenings of the previous day over a cup of tea and a biscuit. It appeared that Ra'ab had manged to hold the mob of pressmen at bay for quite some time, but finally two of the British newspaper reporters had by various promises (unkept, of course) managed to wriggle their way into the house, and had interviewed her in quite an aggressive but persuasive manner. The classic phrase was, "If he plays ball with us and admits he's an imposter we'll give you such a press that the book will sell in millions, you'll never have to worry about money again." Lying ill as he was in another part of the house, he was aware of what was going on. The doctor was sent to fetch Ra'ab to his side. "Get the scum out of here," he told her in a voice barely above a whisper. "Get rid of them and their 'ball.' Tell them to go to hell." Knowing Ra'ab, she probably did not go that far. She was the cautious one of the three of us.

So he received a very unfavourable press from which his image has never recovered. But - and this is the important part - he maintained his position from which he never faltered or varied until the end of his life. He adamantly insisted that his books were true, he was genuine, he was no imposter. He never faltered or wavered from that position, neither in public or private life.

There had been people around the house all day, they went through the dustbins, they crept along the cliff path under his window with mirrors on long poles, they waylaid anyone who approached the house, they tried to stop Dr. B. to interview and photograph him. Then it seems they had combed the village for stories about us all. They were still there at the Cliff Hotel, but by this time their numbers were dwindling. It had fallen as flat for them as my plan to stop them, and they desisted naturally because there was nothing more to say. For three days, I am told, the story held the front pages, then it faded, as scandalous stories always do, leaving behind the debris and detritus for us to live with and overcome. If you were to ask if it made any difference to us being the target of bad publicity, then I would answer yes, it made a lot of difference and in various ways.

On a purely practical level one big disappointment was that the publisher declined any other books. Three more books were actually published in hard cover by another publisher in Britain, but it was a smaller, lesser known firm and there was not the same distribution. There were also translations in other languages, but not on the same scale as for 'The Third Eye.' That, of course, meant less money, and money, distasteful as it may be, was the reason for writing, money needed to do the real work. The reading public at best are fickle, as any writer knows, but now the uncertainty of royalties was a worry, and Chen was not prepared to lecture or appear in public to augment his income as most writers are forced to do. The agent, Cecil Banks, continued to represent Chen until he retired from the firm, and that was a comfort.

As well, it made a difference to the fan mail, which perhaps was a good thing. Now the people who wrote were more serious and therefore not swayed by any bad publicity, but there were far fewer letters than before, although still enough to keep us busy. It was an indication of how powerful the media is in controlling mass thought.

'It must be true – it was in the paper,' people wll say. Often nothing is further from the truth than that which the press are capable of cleverly indicating to a gullible public.

The major difference, however, was within Chen himself. He became more defensive, even more loathe to see people. He had been severely injured. In the long haul, that is, over the years, it may even have impaired his psychic ability, although this was not apparent for a long, long time. He had always been unabe to tolerate superficial sensation seekers, but previously at least he had been civil. Now it seemed he had to be offensive sometimes to keep them away. This was unfortunate because it earned him a poor reputation in certain circles, and it was an unfair and undeserved reputation. Then there was the controversy over who he was. Let me explain how the plumber story originated:

Ra'ab's first husband must have been an interesting man, although I formed the opinion that he was weak in certain ways. I hasten to say that I could be mistaken in that assessment - I never met him, he had long since departed. My understanding was that his father owned a plumbing business in Devonshire, but I doubt very much that either he or his son would have known how to fix the dozens of things that plumbers fix, they left that to their employees. He seems, this first husband, to have been a bit of a misfit. Again, I am guessing because we discussed him very infrequently, but he had a much greater than usual interest in esoteric and metaphysical matters. He was, or so I believe, working with photography to make the aura visible on film, or to relay to the astral, but was having no success and may not even have known consciously why he was doing it or exactly what he was doing. He obviously knew there was something he was supposed to be doing, but was not clear what it was. Unless you are psychic and understand the ability, there is often confusion just like a scrambled telephone line. You are bugged and unhappy all the time because you cannot get through the veil to your Overself and see things clearly, yet you know there is something you should be doing, but what it is - well, that part is unclear. He was depressed and ready to give up. So Chen took his place and allowed him to leave, allowed his kharma to be cleared. Chen took his space, the work had to be done.

That is really all there was to it. We had long discussions about Chen writing a book describing this and explaining the taking over of another body, transmigration, as it is called. He felt it was necessary to tell it as it was. Ra'ab, on the other hand, was opposed to him writing anything of the sort. She expostulated that he would never be believed, the public would think he was completely mad, it just was not the kind of thing you tried to explain to people who were esoterically unaware. I had such faith in Chen that I agreed with him. I reasoned that even if he was not generally believed at that time, he may well be vindicated in the future, and I still believe that to be the case. His way of telling a story was gripping, and could be read by anyone. What the reader got out of it was up to him or her. You could read it as a fantastic story today, tomorrow you might read it as a true and vital account.

The upshot was that he wrote about his experiences after he left Tibet, he wrote about the taking over of another body, and he wrote it in his own inimitable way, the sort of book that one cannot put down because it grabs you and carries you along like a thriller. Whether or not you believe it, you still are compelled to read it. But I have always maintained that, while all his books were best sellers, and he wrote twenty-one at least, only in one, 'The Third Eye,' did he put his heart because after that his heart was broken. That was really what happened as a result of the lies and insinuations about him. It broke his heart, but not his invincible spirit. He continued in face of it all.

Even now, so long after, theories abound about who Lobsang Rampa really was. Some say the books were written by a group of university graduates, others that he was transcribing dictation from the Other Side, and yet others that he was a psychic describing a past life. But the truth is just as he gave it. He may have jazzed it up a bit to make it more readable, but all writers do that. There is nothing to be gained in writing a great work so dull that no one gets beyond the first chapter then, bored to tears, relegates it to the top shelf where it stays forever, unread.

We continued our lives in Ireland for a while. If the locals held anything against us they kept it hidden. The Irish have known so much trouble that they do their best to avoid any more and will appear friendly, and in fact will be genuinely friendly, because they want things to turn out well. Time was running out, however, and we all knew that before long we would be up and away. Chen disliked putting down roots. He needed to be moving and gaining fresh experiences. The thing that finally got us mobilized was that Naughton decided to buy the little stone house on the cliff. Our landlord lived in Sutton Cross and he had had the house up for sale for some time, but with no takers - no takers, that is, until good old Naughton came along with his disruptive way of doing things. It is hard to know what his motives were, whether he was truly altruistic and wanted to assist Chen by giving him a rent free house, or whether he believed that in doing so it would give him power over the situation. As I had no great goodwill towards poor Naughton, I am inclined to believe the latter. Whatever the truth was, Chen announced that if Naughton wanted the house, well and good, but he was not staying there anyway. So that was the end of it, and the end of our contact with Naughton who took offense, saw Chen as ungrateful and exited our lives with no tears on our part, and possibly only temper tantrums on his.

North America was our next goal, really the USA but that was

Habitat

Rampa in bed

Rampa at Habitat

Rampa in motorized wheelchair

Rampa in tibetan clothing

Rampa at railyard

thwarted because Chen had TB scars on his lungs so was unacceptable for immigration to the United States. Canada seemed the obvious choice, and in fact the only other possibility, and we began the long business of filling in papers, undergoing medicals examinations, etc.

Before we left, I wanted to see Lady Shane to say goodbye. She was a person I liked and admired, and I knew she was ill. I went over to the castle one afternoon, and found her lying in her bed, almost a mythical figure. The four poster was huge, the curtains hung frayed and falling to bits, and there was a bedstool placed beside the bed, it was too high to climb into otherwise. The long, narrow windows looked out over what had been park-land, and still was in a sense, and the sun fell in long shafts on the counterpane. Ping lay at her feet, guarding his beloved mistress. Only he and Maggie were there to take care of her in what we both knew was her last illness. She had refused hospital, and managed with the frequent visits of the doctor and the priest.

Her once glowing cheeks were yellowed, the skin pulled tight, her eyes sunken. I had no wish to prolong my visit, it was too tiring for her and too painful for me, but before I left she said, "Your life won't be easy, you know, it never is with a genius, but it will be worth it." I felt a kinship and an under-standing with her such as I seldom find with other people. Although our lives had touched briefly, I felt we had known each other in many, many lives before, and I think we both knew our paths would cross again.

That same day in the evening when I arrived home Ra'ab handed me a letter. It was from Martie and it delighted me to hear from her. I came across her note only the other day amongst my papers: 'Dear Madam: I am taking the liberty of writing to you to tell you that my Neice was very happy with the clothes you said I was to take from your wardrobe. I hope I did right in taking the beautiful red satin you wore for your Presentation. She is going to a Wedding at Southend-on-Sea and will look beautiful in it, quite a lady. I took it up a little and let out the side seams and it fits her very nicely. I often say a little Prayer for you, Madam. God will take care of you. Respectfully yours, Margaret Martin."

And so ended another chapter.

CHAPTER SEVEN

Windsor, Canada. The airport, two days before Christmas, 1959. It was a modest sized airport not intended to take large crowds, but this day it was jammed with people, people loaded with luggage and parcels wrapped in bright shiny paper, people stressed and irritable. The business of Christmas was getting them down, exhausting them. The counter attendant at the buffet was almost at the end of her shift for the day. She had had enough, she could hardly wait to get out of the place and be on her way home.

"Then, just as I'm about to leave, this woman comes along and asks for three cups of tea," the counter attendant told her husband later that evening. "English, looks real done in, but with this voice like she thinks she's the Queen, or something. Well, I told her to help herself. She looks confused, like she doesn't know what I'm talking about, so I get the hot water from the urn for her in the cups. 'No,' she says, real firm, 'I'd like tea, please, not water.' 'Tea bags right there,' I tell her, pointing to them. 'Tea bags?' she says, 'what's that? I'd like tea, not bags.' Imagine! Gee, didn't even know what tea bags were! Don't know what kind of immigrants we're getting these days, sure makes you wonder." Her husband turned up the volume on the telelvision. He wasn't interested in the vagaries of oddballs.

We had been delayed at New York. The small plane sat on the tarmac for at least an hour before it got clearance. "Worst time of year to travel," the pilot had said. "Poor weather conditions, too many travellers, extra planes put on, worst time of year." He was not too happy himself at the thought of taking three adults and two cats to Canada, too much water to fly over for one thing, and the wrong time of year. He would have preferred to be at home instead of battling with the hassle of Christmas. Never mind, it was money in the bank.

At Windsor the formalities seemed to take forever. Eventually, we were through, we were labelled legally Landed Immigrants to this Land of the Free, the New World, Canada. It was stamped on our passports, Landed Immigrant, so it had to be right, that was what we were. But where was the friend who was meeting us? He had given up and gone home, that seemed obvious.

I found the telephones, and after a struggle with the one I had lined up for, having it refuse to do what I wanted and insisting on spitting back the coins I kept putting in, or, alternatively, gobbling up others without putting me through, I reached the friend. His name was Paul. He was an old friend of the Rampa's from London days, well before I knew them. He must have been sitting right beside the telephone, because he answered immediately. "Okay, I'll be there in half an hour," he said with assurance. "Just sit tight."

"Let's have a cup of tea while we wait," Chen suggested. I went to get it but it was disgusting, all you could say for it was that it was warm and wet and a time killer. Ra'ab was much better at doing those kind of things, better able to handle new things than I was, but she was occupied pacifying the cats. And the tea would not have tasted any better even if she had got it instead of me. It would still have been warm water with a bag of dust-like tea thrown in. That must be how they make it in Canada, I thought.

Paul had done his best, and found a house he thought suitable for us all. It was outside Windsor at a place called Tecumseh, right on a lake, Lake St. Claire, opposite Grosse Pointe where the wealthy of Detroit lived. The lake seemed immense, just one huge stretch of frozen water at that time of year, but it was as nothing compared to the Great Lakes, Erie, Huron,

Superior, Ontario and Michigan, which are like inland seas connected to each other.

We stayed there, in Tecumseh, in the snow and ice for a couple of months. Then we moved to Windsor, where we rented a standard riverfront house, right opposite Detroit and not too far from the tunnel under the river. It was near the Ambassador Bridge, too, so we had a choice of over or under the water whenever we went to Detroit for camera equipment, or other needs. Being on the water and close to a major US city were important for Chen, he was in the midst of activity and movement, world progress. That seemed to be what he needed for his work.

Countries, just like people, come under astrological influences. Canada is a Cancer country, the United States of America is Gemini. In general, Americans tend to be talkative, they like change, adore gadgets, are always on the go and like getting ahead. Canadians, on the other hand and, again, only in general, are quieter, modest, home and family lovers, keepers of the peace at all costs because the country is ruled by Cancer. By rights Canada should be a good place for me because my own birth sign is Cancer, but it just simply was not what I expected, or at least the places we lived in were not. One could argue that we were always close to the US border and that certainly may have had a bearing on it. If we had lived in more remote parts it may have been different, but my ideas of what the country was like were based - as with Ireland - on childhood concepts gained from writers like Grey Owl and John Buchan. Where were the log cabins? Where was the grandiose geography, the mountains, prairies, forests, rivers and glaciers? And where were the wild animals and the Red Indians, the true inhabitants of this country? Nowhere to be seen anywhere where we lived. I longed for the untamed parts of this immense country and instead saw only ribbon development with vulgar hoardings advertising, advertising, advertising, everything was money, everything was new and glittering and uncomfortable for me. Nothing was more than skin deep, there was no substance, or that was how it struck me, and I withdrew into my shell. It was different for the others, I think, or maybe they were just more adaptable than I was. Certainly neither of them were Cancer crabs as I am. Chen was Aires, and R'ab on the cusp of Gemini and Taurus.

We stayed in Ontario for around five years, making many moves but always close to the water. When I look at the colours for that time, the colours in my magic painting, they are insipid, dull and uninteresting. Chen continued his life much as it was before, writing, dealing with letters, keeping up with scientific and world affairs. He never intended to be a writer, but that was what he was known as because that is how he made a living – although writing is actually quite a precarious way of making a living. You might put a huge effort into your writing only to find the book or article does not sell. Perhaps the publisher is at fault, perhaps the timing is wrong, perhaps the public just do not like or understand it. Again, the reviewers may not like you, and their opinion exercises great influence over the public.

When it became time for a paperback firm to publish 'The Third Eye,' it was taken by a young company with an editor who proved to be not only interested in Chen's work and to believe in him, but was also invariably agreeable. None of us ever met him, but we wrote hundreds of letters to him, as he to Chen. I say 'we' because we worked as a team. This paperback firm eventually became the principal publisher, and after the first four books nothing was ever printed in hardback again.

Chen felt a certain loyalty to the firm and the publisher, and stayed with them until the end. And the books sold. The sad part is that the cheap paper used in those books disintegrates over time. Now, at the time of writing, I am unable to even open one without experiencing breathing difficulties caused by the chemicals in the paper. Not only that, they are difficult to read because of the yellowing of the paper and the poor print. The hard cover books, on the other hand, are almost as good as new, and completely readable.

Chen routinely discussed things with both Ra'ab and myself. I typed everything from his dictation, and Ra'ab checked it. His ability to include us all always in everything was what kept us together, and gave great strength and stability. We were tightly bound and mixed very little with others. Occasionally I might get my hair done, for instance, and when that happened he preferred not to see me for a few hours afterwards. The aura of the hairdresser lingered around my head or was mixed with my own colours, which he found distressing. "I just don't want to know about that fellow," he would say. He was so accustomed to both of us, Ra'ab and me, that he was able to disregard, or at least accept, our changing colours. But he definitely preferred we did not mix with outsiders other than on a superficial level. This was no hardship to me. I contented myself by taking up painting, needlepoint, reading a lot, and making a thorough and enjoyable study of antiques – rugs, paintings, furniture, silver, all things I loved to experience and later on to own. In the world today we are supposed to mix and be sociable, children have it drummed into them from their earliest days that they need to be one of the crowd, but in fact one can gain far more from remaining solitary. I believe that quietude and self-reliance are not sufficiently valued by the majority. Throughout the years I lived with Chen I was able to indulge that rare state of solitude and it is significant that not once did I visit a doctor, I was never ill, not even with the common cold.

Memories are funny things and it seems odd that my most outstanding memory of Windsor was the monkey. You would think all my attention was focussed on the work we were doing together, Chen, Ra'ab and I, and to a great extent it was, but that was everyday and ongoing. The monkey was different.

I used to walk quite a lot when it was not too hot or too cold, which admittedly was limiting. By this time, however, I was getting used to shedding clothes like a dog shedding its coat in summer, and piling clothes on in winter, which tended to extend the yearly walking period, and on my walks I got to know Windsor well. I always stopped at one particular pet shop just to look in the window, and it was on one of those stops that I saw the monkey. He was sitting in a cramped cage, and a more dejected looking monkey you never saw. I was compelled to enter the shop and was immediately struck by that smell peculiar to a pet shop selling livestock only for profit, a smell made up of wet sawdust, unclean animals and food left for too long in the cages. I enquired the price of the monkey.

"Oh yes, poor little fellow, needs a good home," said the proprietor. "Came from Central America. Needs a good home," he repeated, at the same time naming a price. I went outside again to take a good look at the 'poor little fellow' and he gazed back at me with huge eyes set in a tiny head. Then he covered his head with two long-fingered hands as if he were in the throes of intense misery. He was so human, he was so sad. My heart went out to him.

"Right, I'll take him," I said as I came back in, and the minute the words were out of my mouth I knew it was a mistake. Nevertheless, I thought, what if the monkey had heard and knew what I had said, I had to take him now. Quick as a flash, the shopkeeper wrote out the bill and eased the cage out of the window. He had no intention of letting me change my mind. I looked at my purchase again, and convinced myself I was right to take him after all. How could I leave this small, defenceless creature there in such abject suffering and misery? I had to take him, he was mine come hell or high water.

Carrying the cage along the streets was eventful. If people did not stop to look, they wanted to, and only a form of manners stopped them. As I neared home I was starting to get nervous. I had no problem with Chen's acceptance of the monkey, but what was Ra'ab going to say? I could only imagine. Whenever I returned home from my walks she was invariably the first one I saw. She would be sitting in the living room through which one had to pass to get to the rest of the house. Her habit was not to greet one, a mere nod was the best you could hope for, but today was different. She took one look at the cage. "What on earth is that?" she snapped.

"Its a monkey. I bought him."

"You what?" Incredulous.

"I said, I bought him. Didn't you hear?" I wasn't going to let her bully me, I was determined to keep the monkey, the poor little fellow. He needed a good home, the pet shop man said so.

"What about the cats? Didn't you think of them before you did such a daft thing as buy a monkey. They're nasty little creatures, it'll make life a misery for the cats."

"Look Ra'ab, I can't have a dog because of the cats, and now you're saying I can't have a monkey. Well, I'm going to have him. The cats will just have to get used to him. He needs a good home." I was getting more and more protective of the monkey and determined to stand my ground.

"You're hopeless, Sheelagh. I don't know what Chen's going to say." She did a huge stage sigh and shoulder shrug, it might have been a monster in the cage instead of a poor, innocent little monkey.

Chen's room was upstairs. It had a window looking out over the river from which he could watch shipping passing through the Lakes with their cargo. The lakers were distinct from ocean-going vessels, flat bottomed, but there were also ocean-going ships which had come from the Atlantic through the St. Lawrence Seaway in Quebec. I went upstairs with the monkey in his cage and found Chen sitting cross-legged on his bed, busy carving a piece of lignum vitae, a wonderful old piece, hard and greenish, that he was making into a pendant. He looked up as I approached.

"Hello. Buttercup. You've got a spider monkey!" I knew he was familiar with monkeys from India but I had fancied this was a little different – but perhaps not, at least he knew it was a spider monkey. "They can be naughty little devils, you know. Woolly monkeys are more placid, but then there're bigger." He got up to take a better look at the little creature. "It doesn't look very well. Where did you get it?" He was not in the least perturbed. The monkey was still cramped up and kept covering his head with his hands. He looked the picture of misery.

"Well, you see, Chen, it was in a horrid pet shop. I had to rescue it. I'm sorry, I hope it'll be all right with the cats." I was almost in tears, afraid he might tell me to take it back, having visions of camping out on the river bank with the monkey in tow.

"Of course you had to get it, you couldn't leave it there. It probably needs something to eat, a piece of banana perhaps. I expect it came from Brasil or somewhere. Trouble is, they catch them very cruelly, sometimes they never recover mentally. Anyway, let's give it a try." Ku'ei had left her safe place and taken cover under the bed. Fifi was out of the way in Ra'ab's room. He considered the situation for a minute then said, "I know, we'll let it out on the sunporch. It can't get away there." Obviously he was not going to assume it was a meek little thing ready for a petting. We took the cage out to the sunporch, which was a sort of addition to his bedroom, faced west and got lots of warmth and light. The windows, as all windows in Ontario, had screens in an attempt to keep mosquitoes and other noxious insects away, so we were able to open the windows without fear of the monkey getting out and creating havoc on the rooftops.

We put the cage down, and I opened the door. Instantly the little thing leapt out screaming and cursing, running around the walls almost at ceiling height, grabbing anything he could, swinging with those amazing long arms. He was utterly wild and furious, terrifying in his rage and frustration. Even Chen was surprised at the power of his fury and his energy. "We'd better leave him and see if he settles down. Can you get out of the door without letting him out and get him something to eat and drink?" he asked.

Gingerly I made my escape when the monkey was at the other end of the sunporch, and came back with carrots, nuts and banana, and a bowl of water.

Ra'ab had been alerted by all the screaming, and watched in disbelief. She actually loved animals, but a monkey was rather beyond her, mainly because of her concern for the cats. "You can't possibly keep that creature," she said with her customary and irritating commonsense. "It's going to upset the cats, not to mention Chen."

"Well, Chen isn't upset. The poor little fellow needs a good home," I told her, inanely repeating the pet shop man's words. "I wish you'd just shut up, Ra'ab." She was not pleased, and was obviously going to be an adversary. "We're going to call him Chuli," I told her, as if having a name made him a reality and a fixture in our household

"That's not what I'd call him," she said flatly. "He's a horror."

Over the next few weeks we tried everything we could think of to accommodate the monkey. We had a carpenter build a very large cage in the sunporch, complete with branches for him to swing on, a sleeping shelf, a feeding area, the works. He still hated us, he hated us intensely and made his hatred known. Whenever I tried to pick him up he bit and screeched. At the crack of dawn he started chattering and screaming. In a way, his agility and wildness was exhilarating, but his hatred was different because it was so destructive. I had always had pets - everything from horses, to dogs, cats, rabbits, fish, birds, tortoises, so I was no stranger to them, but over the weeks I was forced to admit that the monkey, as Ra'ab had predicted, would have to go. There was no likelihood that he was going to subject himself to domesticity, and besides his distrust of humans was all-consuming.

The day came when I admitted defeat. We had acquired an old American car, and I waited until the others were out for a run and then, with a heavy heart, enticed him into his tiny cage. I left the house on foot and took him to the nearest veterinarian to have him euthanised. It is always a difficult decision, but in this case there was no other way, I was convinced of it. Even if he could have been returned to the jungle, he was far too damaged to ever recover his sanity. Poor little fellow, the pet shop man was right. But why, I wonder, do we keep doing it to animals? Why do we see them as objects for our pleasure? They are not. They are different from us, but they have the same right to the Earth as we have.

With Chuli gone the house returned to normal. Everyone was sympathetic although I never really forgot the 'poor little fellow.' But he had need of more than a good home, much more. He needed what civilization could never return to him because, in our insane obsession and lust for power and money we have lost it ourselves - we have lost our freedom.

* * *

Chen had an astonishing knowledge of world affairs on all levels. He knew about the hippie movement, he knew about world leaders and politics, science, mechanics, art, medicine. He was up to the minute on current trends and crazes, the way the masses were swayed, the way they thought, pop music and things like that, the common side of life as well as the elite. The Beatles, Elvis Presley, and all the rest of it. He had lived and experienced life in diverse places in different societies, all the time observing, but now he observed and listened in a more sedantary manner. Photography was still a major interest, but his focus shifted during those early years in Canada to radio. He had powerful shortwave radios that could tune in to virtually anywhere in the world if you had time to fiddle and knew how to do it. Oh, but he was deaf, you will be saying, how could he listen? He listened in two ways – by placing his fingers on the set and picking up through vibration, and through wearing a headset and picking up by bone conduction. It needed concentration, though. As well as short waves we had ham and police radios which were often amusing, sometimes exciting and enlightening. But for relaxation he listened with his fingers to what I would call light classical music.

During that period I came to understand how disease can be cured, made into ease, or health, by colour and/or sound which are, after all, vibrations. Disease, or imminent disease, causes a faulty vibration in the organ affected and results in a murky colour in the aura which is the indication of illness. By correcting that vibration, the colour can be restored and good health can be recovered. Fifty years ago these concepts were too advanced to be accepted, but now it is a different matter, and there is hope for the future. Perhaps, after all, a better solution than transplants will be reached by scientists. Progress has been made, Chen laid valuable foundations which are coming to fruition now forty or fifty years later. If there was a serious problem anywhere in the world Chen was focussed on it. He would work with his hands carving or painting because he maintained that working with one's hands helps to focus thought, and thought can be a very powerful tool for influencing events.

After perhaps a couple of years in Tecumseh and Windsor it was time to move again. Truthfully I cannot remember exactly which move followed which while we were in Ontario, the sequence of it all escapes me. I do remember, however, that we lived on the Niagara Parkway for a time in a sort of holiday cottage place. It was winter, the cottages were not used at that time of year, and the owner of the place rented her own house to us for those sub-zero months. It was a pleasant enough house, not unlike the German lady's flat we had rented first in London in that it was over-furnished for us, and we put away most of her things while we were there.

We had a small car by this time instead of the large American creature, and would drive around, sometimes to Niagara Falls or St. Catherine's, or in the other direction to Fort Erie and beyond. The spray from the falls would cover the trees and, because it was so cold, was instantly frozen. To see the trees at night bathed in icicles was quite a marvellous sight, more wonderful to me than the falls itself, even though they were themselves indeed impressive.

At some point we moved to Fort Erie. It was there that another stroke of bad publicity hit. A teenage boy in Brighton, England, had killed himself and his mother loudly proclaimed that it was the Rampa books that killed him. Once again, we had the press from Britain and Canada to contend with, this time we were more prepared, more calm, and outwardly less concerned. It did have the effect of bringing us together even more closely. Hardship will do that.

The problem seemed to have arisen from a book Chen had had published as a course on metaphysics and esoteric practices for serious students of the occult. It was intended for a limited audience, but even so was very, very carefully written to include only directions and practices which were entirely safe for the amateur to engage in alone, in other words, without the presence of an Adept or Master. Some of the more advanced practices can be dangerous if undertaken without skilled supervision, but these latter, as I say, were definitely not included in the course which became a book. It was for private circulation at first, but then seemed so valuable that the paperback publisher was anxious to publish it, and thus it was that this mother whose son had killed himself was accusing 'the Rampa books.' She had found a copy of the course in her son's room. The mother, no doubt distraught and ignorant of esoterics, blamed the book rather than anything else which may have been going on with her son.

Fort Erie was a small town, and after the newspaper reports about 'the killer book,' reports full of sensation such as we had come to expect from the press, especially the British press which must be the most sensational in the world, one would be walking down the street only to find that the sidewalk was suddenly entirely deserted, everyone had crossed to the other side and was studiously looking the other way!

Book sales suffered too. For a time it was difficult to make ends meet. We moved to a ramshackle place above the local Salvation Army shop. It was another winter, and a cold one, and I remember how the small windows were so frozen over with snow and ice that one could barely see out. The heating arrangements were minimal, in any case we had no money for satisfactory heating, and simply piled on clothes and thick socks and boots. I shopped at the local supermarket, and thank heavens for the bargain tray – things which were slightly out-dated but perfectly edible, old bread which was fine for toast, milk not yet gone off, fruit and vegetables only a little past their prime.

My recollection of Christmas that year (not that we kept Christmas but there was the usual work-up to the holiday which was impossible to avoid) was feasting on an entire bag of rather overripe apples which had cost no more than a couple of dollars. The sense of virtue was cancelled by the tummy ache that followed in its wake!

There is a saying about kicking a dog when he is down, and I have to believe there is more than a grain of truth in that sentiment. I am thinking of another unpleasant affair in Fort Erie, and quite memorable for its unpleasantness. We were raided by the Mounties, the Royal Canadian

Mounted Police, one of the symbols of Canada. Doubtless, they can be and are heroic keepers of the peace, but we saw them in quite a different light at that time. They seem to particularly police USA/Canada border points – and Fort Erie was just that, a small border town on the other side of the river from Buffalo, New York, that was why we lived there - and we were unlucky enough to come under RCMP scrutiny for a quite minor transgression.

We had moved to a slightly better place after the Salvation Army shop, or rather above it, but the new place was still far from being a haven of comfort and splendour, it was the sort of place people look down their noses at with contempt. We were never disturbed by that attitude as a rule, it just happened that that was a major factor in the way the RCMP treated us.

We had rented two apartments next door to each other, mine being virtually one room, the others occuping what was classified as a one bed-room suite. We were fair game, in a way, for the Mounties, what with the press trouble causing locals to see us as suspect, and then the cheap places we lived in. And then again, the apartment block was very close to the bridge leading to Buffalo, perfect for smugglers, one could reason. All in all, we must have presented a strange picture to the police who are not remarkable for their powers of imagination at the best of times, and they may well have had their eye already on us when someone sent them an anonymous letter (so we later discoverd) accusing us of smuggling goods over the border. It was just what they needed, now they could investigate these odd-balls living in their midst.

No matter how innocent one is, how free of guilt, no one likes the police arriving on their doorstep, especially the Mounties in border towns where they are out to get you, and I was no exception to that rule. I can see them again in my mind's eye, four – yes, four – larger than life characters almost out of a movie. My door was the first of our two doors they reached after climbing the rather grubby stairs to the first floor where we lived, and I happened to be washing my hair at that moment when they started banging on the door - not knocking, banging. There is a difference. Good God, I thought, there must be a fire, someone must have been murdered, the place must be falling down to warrant all that racket, so I grabbed a towel and wound it round my sudsy head, rubbing the soap out of my eyes as I hastened to answer that infernal din.

What confronted me threw me into a complete tizzy. I would love to say that I treated them with scornful disdain, that I kept my cool and most of all my dignity, but, alas, no, that was not the way it was. If I had been in England on my own ground it might have been different, but here in Canada I was at the very bottom of the pile, by Canadian standards I was a nobody, I had no money, no university education, no ability to do anything that counted for anything in this country. I was swept under the carpet, and by this time was beginning to truly feel like a third rate citizen. After all, we had lived in Canada for a good many years by now, and it does catch up.

Here I was then, wet hair, soap in my eyes, shaking with fright being shown some kind of card by this large intimidating policeman flanked by three others, equally as large and menacing. "No," I said, "Dr. Rampa doesn't live here." Seeing they were about to push me aside and enter, I weakly said, "He's next door," stepped back and shut my door. What a coward! I comfort myself with the knowledge that they would very quickly have realised we had two apartments, whatever else they may have been, they were not fools.

The question is, did Chen smuggle goods from the USA, did he bring things over the border without declaring them? The answer is no, he did not. He insisted that we declare everything, he was too used to trouble to want to have any more. Sometimes duty was charged, sometimes it was not, but all his equipment was declared. There had been a person who volunteered to bring back a typewriter in his car for us, as we had no car at that time, and it was awkward on the bus, and although he had been instructed to declare it, he pooh-poohed the idea. No, no, he insisted, he was used to getting stuff through without duty, just leave it to him. It was awkward and impossible to explain that we would prefer to pay the extra money because money was like God to him. Other than that, I was the prime culprit. I often bought clothing, make-up, little things, and did not declare them. My excuse is that everyone did the same. If we had made declarations all the time it would have held up the bus and just been a nuisance. Besides, how trivial it all was in the scheme of things. It was not my little things – although they took everything – it was Chen and his technical, scientific things they were after, and they confiscated everything for which he could not produce proof of payment. We were careless about keeping such things, never liking to be cluttered with what seemed unnecessary. They ransacked the two apartments as though they were dogs trained to sniff things out, but I would have preferred dogs any day. They were ruthless and crude, and utterly shattered my ideals of the wonderful Mounted Police. Scotland Yard – well, they had a different approach altogether. To have been investigated by the cream of police of England and Canada is a dubious claim to fame, and one I would prefrer not to make, but alas I am obliged to.

* * *

Ever since I had known him Chen's health had been, if not delicate, dicey. He had enormous muscular or bodily strength, but his back had been damaged, his jaws had been kicked while in prisoner-of-war camp in Japan, and now caused him pain and discomfort, as well as disfiguration which his beard hid to some extent, and his hearing was almost totally gone. He had much to cope with, and although he seldom complained he required a lot of rest and care. But it was while we were living over the Salvation Army shop that the first major problem with his walking occurred. I so specifically remember it only because we found a pair of crutches in the shop costing very little, and he started to use them. Whether he had an accident or whether it was natural degeneration, I am not sure now, but I distinctly remember his asking me to search the shop for crutches.

Everyone probably knows what a thrift shop is like, and a lot of people would never dream of going into one and rummaging through the mountains of rubbish in the hopes of unearthing something useful, or even nice. I cannot say I am exactly a fan of thrift shops myself, but sometimes necessity is more than the mother of invention, and when you are charged with finding a certain thing it makes the task a lot simpler. The woman who looked after the shop was sour, and so might I be in her place, it must be dismal to be surrounded by unsaleable stuff all and every day. And to her we were just 'those people that live upstairs,' and therefore not much different than what she was custodian to. It was all junk anyway, stuff thrown out, not much use to anyone.

"Good morning! Do you have any crutches?" I brightly enquired.

She was sitting at the back of the shop huddled over the heater with a mug of coffee on the floor and a stack of old magazines by her side which she was obviously wading through. She looked up reluctantly. "What's that you want?" she said. "I don't know what you mean, but you can look if you want. Looking's free." She went back to her magazines.

"Crutches, you know, wooden things to support you if you've broken a leg or something." I wasn't too thrilled at the thought of rummaging if she knew where such a thing might be.

Light seemed to dawn. "I don't know. You're really hard to understand, you know, its that accent you've got. As I said, take a look. I'm busy." She got back to the magazines.

So I looked, and just as I was giving up I saw a black rubber tip sticking out from under a fold-up bed, and lo and behold it was a crutch. Its pair had to be somewhere, and in a matter of minutes I found it. I took the two crutches to her triumphantly. "Look, isn't that wonderful, you've got the exact thing I'm looking for! I hope they're the right size."

"Oh, those. Let's see, where's the price?" We both looked but found nothing. "Oh well, you can take them for five dollars. I guess no one else will want them."

So Chen got his crutches and showed me how you put your weight on your forearms, not on your shoulders as seems the obvious thing to do. He used them around the house sporadically, and it probably delayed the day he was oobliged to get a wheelchair, which came a number of years later.

Throughout the time we were in difficult straits financially there were a number of people who helped. They realised that humanity owed a debt to those like Chen. They were well evolved people, concerned for the welfare of our Earth, and Chen accepted their help. It was not altogether the material part of it, it was the confidence expressed by these individuals that was important. It was a confirmation that what he was attempting was worthwhile, even though the odds were heavily balanced in favour of the negative side.

One of the people who was constant and wrote long letters dealing with a variety of subjects was from South America. All the books were translated into the Spanish language and were best sellers, even though we had never received royalties from the publisher in Argentina. It was an issue because we badly needed what was owing in order, not only to continue with the work, but for basic survival. No amount of correspondence with the publisher produced anything except excuses, although the books went on being translated and sold. So when our South American correspondent broached an idea which normally would have been abhorrent to Chen, he was obliged to consider it.

The plan was that a club would be formed under the name of 'Los Amigos de Lobsang Rampa' and we would all go to Montevideo with the idea that Chen would teach and advise the group. It was supposedly comprised of wealthy people prepared to pay our way and see we were looked after in their country. Initially, Chen rejected the idea point blank. Having a group under his name did not appeal in the least, in fact he was strongly opposed to it. But as time went on, and our correspondent became more vociferous, more insistent and more convincing, he began to come round to the idea that perhaps we had no choice, perhaps he would have to comply with what they wanted, making it clear that it was a temporary arrangement only. Perhaps it would enable him to retrieve the monies owing from Argentina. So, to cut a rather long story short, he decided that we would go.

Partly because of the cats and partly because it seemed the best way, we finally decided to travel by cargo boat from New York. Flying with the cats from Ireland had been a nightmare; we had come to Canada by Swiss Air as they had agreed to take the cats in the cabin with us provided we travel first class, the only airline we approached who offered us that choice, all the others insisting on the cats travelling in the hold where animals habitually travelled. Despite a shot of something-or-other intended to calm them, it had the opposite effect and they caused an horrific hullabaloo on the flight, yowling their heads off as only Siamese cats can do. Ra'ab and I were forced to take it in turns to sit in a tiny area at the rear of the plane with them in order to pacify the other first class passengers. We had no desire to repeat that performance. A sea passage to South America was enticing, and the choice of a cargo boat over a liner highly appealing as they carried no more than twelve passengers, calling at a number of ports en route.

And so it was decided. It was December and we would be sailing towards the sun, leaving North America, which held few joyous memories for me, far behind. I was excited at the prospect. Ra'ab studiously studied Spanish. I refused to, and actually had no reason to regret my laziness because we were to find that in general South Americans were more anxious to learn English than listen to our fractured Spanish.

It was the year of the 'Bay of Pigs.' Americans were not travelling or taking holidays anywhere near Cuba, therefore we were the only passengers on the quite modern and comfortable Moore McCormack cargo ship. Apart from a tragic event when we encountered a raging storm off the coast of South Carolina, the voyage was a tonic, and as we sailed further south and the weather improved, it was altogether enjoyable. There was the added attraction of a swimming pool on deck of which I was the exclusive user.

The Captain was a well-rounded, jolly soul and in keeping with the predilection for giving nicknames peculiar to Chen, he became Billy Bunter to us. After dinner Captain Billy would descend from the bridge to Chen's stateroom, make himself at home, and we would join in a singsong together. He had an impressive and extensive catalogue of sea shanties at his command and would boom them out in a strong bass voice, beating time on his knee, first making us join in the chorus and later teaching us the verses. We returned the visit by going up to the bridge and examining the equipment and workings of a sea captain's life. Because of our tragedy I came to feel a special respect and closeness to him.

Fifi Greywhiskers was, if truth were to be told, too old to undertake a sea voyage of any length, but she was part of the family and it would have been unthinkable to leave her behind, even in the most benign and cosy situation. Where one of us went, we all went. My impression was that Chen felt himself to be in a borrowed position – as he was – and he had to work at it to keep it going, to keep his life a solid reality, and he relied on the unity of the family to keep it intact. So Fifi came along on the voyage, and had it not been for the storm all might have been well.

When the ship began to roll and toss and everything that was not secured started to move, chairs careening from side to side of the staterooms in a crazy dance, things, books, anything, tumbling down, and, added to the general racket and cacophany of wind and waves, the clanging of the ship, the moaning and groaning of its structure, we were as good as in bedlam. Fifi became ill, very ill. Chen and Ra'ab did what they could for the little creature, but what could they do except to calm her? From this distance of many years afterwards it is hard to say how long the storm lasted, it might have been a day and a night, it might have been two days, or more. However long it was it seemed interminable. Just as one felt it was abating a little, the worst happened. Fifi received a blow from a piece of furniture. If only it had been fatal - but it was not. She was concussed, she seizured, she was visibly suffering, she was at the end but was still alive.

The Captain was sent for and, amazingly, he came despite being in the throes of the storm and having to take care of his ship, his crew and his passsengers - his passengers, well, we were his passengers after all, so he was only doing his duty by coming - but although he carried medications for humans he was not permitted to use them to relieve animals. "We only need a little morphine, enough to help her to go," we begged him, but it was no use. "You'll have to put her overboard," he said. Plain as words he was thinking it was only a cat, after all, it was half dead, it had to be drowned and finished off, nothing else for it. Why could we not just get on with it? He was, of course, perfectly right although when one is closely and emotionally connected to an animal it is not so easy.

Buddhists, as we all know, do not take life but Chen was a humanitarian, a free thinker and he assidiously followed the Middle Way. He never adhered utterly, blindly and strictly to any rule because he knew there was always the exception, rules are made to be broken when necessity and intelligence demand. He knew Captain Billy was right in what he was clearly thinking. Fifi was unconscious but still alive, she had to be let go. In plain language, she had to be drowned while unconscious. He looked at Ra'ab, she looked at him. Something seemed to pass between them.

"Can you get a sack and weights?" Chen asked the Captain, his face expressionless.

"Yes, but I can't do it, I can't put the cat over. One of you will have to do it." Captain Billy was a practical man and his company had rules. It was not that he was uncaring, it was simply that his mind was on keeping his ship afloat, not on some small cat who meant nothing to him. He looked at us enquiringly, he wanted to get this over with. Chen and Ra'ab remained silent. There was only one person to do it, one person not so closely attached as the other two, and I was that person. Obviously. I had to do it, there was no other way and it was pointless to dilly dally. Get on with it, let the Captain get back to his duties.

"I'll do it," I said, "But will you come with me, Captain?"

And so Chen carefully and lovingly wrapped the little cat in a towel. She was far gone and unaware but her breathing was gasping and laboured. If only she would die now, I thought, but it was not to be. She was placed in the weighted sack and the two of us, myself and the Captain, took that pathetic bundle, that cold damp sack containing Fifi Greywhiskers, her heart still beating although she was senseless, to the deck rail. We made our way from below up the ladder. It is every man for himself in a storm, if you hang onto someone else you can bring them down with you. Captain Billy carried the sack. He had brought rain gear, the sort worn by seamen, heavy oilskin and sou'wester, to cover and protect me, and he stayed behind me in case I fell. We reached the rail, the biting wind and sharp rain in our faces, the cruel black sea churning and roiling below, gigantic, terrifying waves, the grey sky a mass of skudding, lowering clouds, the ship dipping and rolling with each capricious upheaval of the ocean. He handed me the sack. Feeling sick and dizzy, I dropped it over. I stood for a moment gazing into that black, bottomless mass, that cruel, heartless, cold grave, then I turned to look at him. He solemnly saluted and then shook my hand. He understood, even in the midst of that storm, saddled with the responsibility for the lives of so many of us as well as for his ship, he had time to understand.

I had steeled myself to send Fifi to her death, I had drawn the hard shell of practicality around me shutting out emotion, it was his caring that brought tears to my eyes and caused a lump to rise in my throat.

I condone euthanasia. I view it as altogether civilized, humane and compassionate to release a soul from a tortured, agonized body, so why does it haunt me still, the dropping of that weighted sack into the relentless sea below? If I had been able to administer a lethal injection and witness the little creature die a painless immediate death instead of the way it was, it may have been different. But there was no other way, and it still lies heavily on my heart.

The storm over we sailed on. Ra'ab coped with the grief of losing Fifi better than expected, her belief sustaining her. Chen - one never knew just how deeply he was affected by sorrow. He carried the sorrow of the world in his heart, I sometimes thought, he saw it, recognised it, carried it. And so, like all those who are acquainted with great sorrow, he was beyond displaying emotion. Undoubtedly, too, he was in touch in the astral, beyond the veil of death.

We sailed down to Central America, on to South America. At each port Ra'ab and I went ashore and looked around, but Chen preferred to stay aboard and watch the loading and unloading, the huge cranes operating, the organization that went into it all. He liked chatting with the first mate who was in charge of the cargo, with the radio officer and the chief engineer. He was in his element and it was as a holiday for him because none of these people had the least idea he was a writer, and would not have had a inkling about, and probably no interest in, anything to do with esoteric or occult subjects, anyway.

We made landfalls at several ports before Rio, some really small and others bustling. It was hot and humid on dry land, and it was always with relief that we set sail once more and headed out to the open sea. We were in warm waters now and the ship cut through the waves, the engine thudding, the ship vibrating to the force, the winds hot and dry. Seabirds wheeled and circled overhead, following the ship, hoping for food. The occasional whale showed himself, a huge fish surfaced and leapt, only to disappear again under the waves, and there were shoals of smaller fish darting through the water like silver flashes. The moon hung in a clear blue-black sky, the sun rose over the horizon. Being away from land on the open sea offered a unique form of freedom, different from flying, better. It was entirely possible to get things in their correct perspective.

As we departed the ports the ship was taken out by one or two small but immensely powerful tug boats until we were safely away, the ropes could be cast off and we were free to get under way. Chen would settle down to dictation then. He was writing another book and I suspect he did some excellent work while on the water. It was planned that I would transcribe those tapes when we arrived at our destination, but alas, they were stolen along with his recording machine when we were in the port of Rio de Janeiro. We had been warned not to leave our staterooms open when in port, but someone had come in through the porthole and removed his radio, as well as the tapes and recorder. What was doubly annoying was that now he felt time was wasted until we reached Uruguay when he would be able to get a further supply of tapes and another recording machine. On the positive side, he had an enforced rest; no mail reached us during those three weeks, and now he was prevented from writing, so there was no option but to resign himself to it.

Finally the day arrived when we sailed up the River Plate, that river which separates Uruguay from Argentina. One would have thought it logical to call at Montevideo first, but instead we went to Buenos Aires to unload cargo, the plan being to make a stop at Montevideo on the return journey for loading. For some reason we were held up in Buenos Aires for several days, it may have been because it was Christmas, or perhaps there was a dockers' strike, I do not recall exactly what it was but it happened. I can remember well, though, the frantic messages being received by the radio officer from our over-wrought sponsor across the River Plate – where were we, when would we arrive, were we really there? The radio officer would come down from his minute cabin, where he spent his days trapped to his headphones, and hand us the messages, one after the other. It was alarming, and we were dreading some form of royal welcome when we did eventually disembark in Montevideo. We left Buenos Aires and, with a sense of foreboding, put ourselves in order for disembarking, however, it was not to be for a few more days. We anchored at some distance outside the harbour of Montevideo and lay there for three days and three nights in sight of our future home.

Our sponsor and the most prominent members of the group, unable to delay a moment longer for the long-awaited meeting with he whom they saw as their guru (a concept which Chen disliked intensely and was to disaffirm), managed to get brought over to the ship in a liberty boat, one of those small boats used for transporting the crew back and forth between land and sea when a ship was forced to anchor outside the harbour. Ra'ab and I stood on the deck waiting to greet them and take them to Chen in his stateroom, and I remember seeing them climb up the ladder one by one. Jaime, the leader and our correspondent, came first. The top of his head was balding, his shoulders were broad. I was expecting a middle-aged man both from the tone and content of his letters and from this first, almost aerial, view of him from the deck as he ascended the ladder, but as his face appeared I saw with astonishment that he was young, probably no more than in his mid to late twenties. He had a small, neat black moustache and a round cherubic face. He was well dressed but one assumed it was in honour of the occasion. He was assured, and shook hands with a slight bow, somehow reminiscent of an elderly European statesman, and spoke in excellent English, constantly clearing his throat. I found him intriguing from the first.

Closely following Jaime came his wife, Angelica, a long limbed, darkly exotic beauty. Her black hair was long and straight, loosely framing her lovely oval face with its lively brown eyes and glistening, smooth complexion. She had not a word of English, but her manner was altogether charming, the more so because she was seemingly unaware of her beauty and charm, it was utterly natural to her. The other two who comprised this first meeting were oddly mismatched, although it was later apparent that they had no connection with each other beyond their common interest in the group. Theresa was sophisticated and attractive in a much more worldly sense than Angelica. She was expensively dressed, but elegantly casual, her perfume was marvellously subtle and trailed in her wake compellingly, her English was sketchy but perfectly comprehensible. It seemed, even at first glance, that she felt herself important for some reason, and it transpired that this was absolutely correct as she was the mistress of a wealthy man, important in the running of the country, who had largely financed this dream of hers, to have the lama teach her personally. Without her friend's input – in which she had persuaded him – it would not have been possible to bring Chen – and all of us – to Montevideo.

The fourth member was a musician. His name was Jorge. He arrived on deck last, and with much ado, as though he had scarcely been able to make it, but he was laughing, full of fun and friendliness. Long, curly dark hair, skin tanned to a deep mahogany by the sun, and a plump, comfortable body, he was the kind of person one immediately felt it would be nice to be around. He, like Angelica, had no English at all, and as we got to know him better amused himself by teaching me utterly incorrect Spanish, sending everyone into stitches of laughter as I solemnly asked them to have 'pan negro' while handing the white bread, assuring them they were 'mis enemigos' as I smiled in a friendly way. If I had thought for a moment I would have known better, but at least it amused everyone and broke the ice. At this first meeting, the first meeting with the lama he so wished to impress, he was correct in manner, but was his own loose, untidy self, which was really a large part of his charm.

These, then, were the first four. They crowded into the stateroom and greeted Chen with hushed reverence. It was hard for him to have four complete strangers at such close quarters, but only Ra'ab and I were aware of how hard; no one would have had any idea that he was almost totally deaf and in fact under great strain. He partly relied on the two of us for comprehension, by which I mean that by watching our reactions and our understanding of the conversation he was more easily able to follow the gist of it. In this case lip reading was virtually useless as even Jaime's enunciation was uniquely his own and it took a little while for Chen to get accustomed to it. The four of them were avid readers of Chen's books, and had interest and understanding of esoterics, so it was obvious that they would sense his difference. And they were awed, they visibly felt the different and powerful vibration emanating from him, and one could see they realised they were in the presence of a higher entity. I found it fascinating because for the most part the people we had met in North America had been much more materialistic and generally lacking in spiritual perception, and it said something about the difference between the cultures – the one considering themselves the rich progressive leaders of the world, the other the dreamers, the ones aspiring to spiritual rather than material gains. I felt I was going to integrate easily and happily, and indeed I did. It was the start of a good period for me, although for Chen it was not entirely easy.

This initial meeting, then, was relatively brief, under an hour, and by that time the four of them were drained emotionally, and Chen was exhausted mentally. Ra'ab, seeing this, intervened and suggested they leave. Jaime took his leave graciously and with much ceremony, assuring us he would be there on the quay when the ship docked the following day, and would take us to the house they had rented for us just outside the city. It had been a good meeting, it boded well, and we went to our bunks that night feeling content, although perhaps a little sorry our sea voyage was over.

When I look at the magic painting I see it coming together now, I see the story shaped, and I can see the end although, in truth, there never really is an end, just an eternal journey, the endless round of existence, on and on.

CHAPTER EIGHT

At the beginning of last week it was my birthday. It was one of those milestone birthdays, and people sent or brought me flowers. They seemed to know I like white, and our tiny house was filled with white flowers. Today, I re-arranged the flowers, taking out and discarding the dead ones, roses, stocks, those small pompom daisies, and putting back the white and cream lilies in clean, fresh water. The perfume is heady and heavy and fills the house. I enjoy the scent and the flowers because they were presents from friends, but when I think about it seriously I know I shall be glad when the lilies, too, are gone and the house returns to normalcy. Yet twenty, fifteen, or even ten years ago I filled my house with flowers religiously every week, I went out to buy them, if there were no flowers the place felt bare and unfriendly, it was somehow lacking. The point I am making is that it brings home to me how we change, and how we forget the way we were at different times of our lives until something happens to jolt the memory, and then things reach back to us out of oblivion, small things, the fine lines. I had forgotten how much I needed flowers.

Is it the same with my story, have I forgotten the fine lines after all these years? Is my magic painting too broad, too full of the big, bold strokes and lacking in the details? How can I tell? When the painting is finished and transcribed into words things will perhaps come back to me that I had forgotten. But maybe, after all, the broad picture is the thing, maybe it is the best I can do.

I have in my mind the overall image of life in Montevideo as being quite charming. I have the sense of relaxation, warmth, colour. I recall sitting on the crowded buses, squashed up tight in a corner with more people riding the bus than would ever be permitted on one vehicle by law – but whoever worried about the law in Montevideo? Hardly anyone. People were jumping on and off the buses, jostling each other, forgetting to pay their fare, laughing and chattering in a language foreign and quite unintelligible to me. I was an onlooker, an outsider. I was of their world, but at the same time not of it, remote but involved. I found it delightful, like being in some wonderland. I remember the European feel of the city without its being European, the beaches, the friendly and easy ways of the people, the musicians on the street, the tango music everywhere, in the bars, in the houses, the shops, that unique music and singing which is so typical to that area. I remember, too, the poverty, but somehow it was not so utterly miserable, hopeless and depraved as in North America, even the beggars appeared more optimistic, it was just their way of life which they accepted, they saw no end to it, so they made the best of it. Perhaps, too, the belief in better things beyond this life permeated even the street life.

The broad picture of life in Montevideo must have been rather different for Chen, and also for Ra'ab. I was the one who went out and did the shopping, collected the mail, mixed with the ordinary people and enjoyed each day. They were treated almost like magicians in a travelling show, kept exclusive, remaining indoors, taking taxis whenever they went out. With hindsight it must have been onerous for both of them, although things did improve as time went on.

As good as his word, Jaime was there waiting for us when the ship docked and we walked down the gangplank for the last time. We were bundled into his car, an antiquated but well maintained black Riley. Angelica was with him, so it was a tight fit, but we drove off in state and followed the course that he had obviously carefully mapped out as being the most scenic, the one with most landmarks. It was hot and it was Christmas, and I would rather have given the sights a miss and got a move on so we could reach the house and let Ku'ei out of her basket But it was not to be. We crawled along, being shown all the points of interest, trying to show enthusiasm, but – it was a trial of endurance! Sightseeing was honestly not my thing. The house they had chosen was beyond the city several miles, I would estimate five or six, and was situated in a type of city seaside, not a resort because it was too close to the city, but a place where people went to sit on a not very pleasant beach, and paddle in not very pleasant water, by which I mean it was a grey, gritty sand, and an even greyer ocean. There were rows of houses, villa type, going up from the beach, and we must have been in the sixth or seventh row back. The group had no idea, naturally, of what would suit Chen, but they could hardly have made a worse choice, and it was not too long before we moved into the city to live in a modern block of flats overlooking the sea.

Angelica turned out to be, as her name implied, quite an angel. We managed to communicate by signs, much laughter, and intuition. Whereas her husband was a pseudo-intellectual, and had no wish to deal with the tiresome business of daily living, Angelica was practical, tireless in her efforts to make us comfortable, see we had suitable food, and even made excellent lightweight black mandarin type jackets for Chen which he adopted as his form of dress for the rest of his life. Without her ministration and concern we would have been in a sorry state. She had little or only superficial interest in the group; it was her husband's baby, and she did all she could to make it a success, not for love of matters esoteric, but for love and duty to her husband. She was a gem.

Jaime was really an entrepreneur with a taste for the unusual. The only child of wealthy parents, he had never had to earn his living or do a day's hard work. He appeared to have unlimited funds supplied by his mother. In this and in other ways, he bore a vague resemblance to Proust, even his appearance was similar, although he was fuller in the face and of a somewhat heavier build. He was, in fact, of French origin. He was a good and convincing writer and could spend hours agonizing over small things. One would constantly be left with the uncomfortable feeling that he had a hidden reason or answer to any query, something he did not wish to divulge. He was naturally secretive, less than straightforward, and could tie himself in knots quite easily. There was a markedly Peter Pan side to him, and from time to time it surfaced in the most astonishing manner, a high pitched, inappropriate giggle, making silly faces behind peoples' backs, stupid things that were supposed to be funny - but were not.

He was deeply and genuinely thoughtful, and searched unremittingly for the meaning of life. Above all, he was determined to make this venture a success, and never, ever to upset the central figure – Chen. Although Chen did not dislike him, he saw through him, and it was difficult sometimes to appear believing of him, knowing he was essentially evasive and misleading in an effort, as Jaime mistakenly saw it, to keep us happy.

At the beginning, members of the group were brought to the house to meet Chen. There were perhaps ten or twelve of them, and from the start they were made to understand that group meetings were not possible. Whether they were aware of Chen's hearing difficulty or not, I do not remember, but they arrived in twos or threes, generally later in the day. I was seldom present, although I was introduced to most of them. Ra'ab would be there, Jaime and often Angelica , and they might stay for a couple of hours or under. The principal player, the one who had largely financed Jaime's scheme, only made himself known after several weeks. He was quite obviously not the least bit interested in Chen or his books at the beginning, his main purpose being to keep his mistress happy and occupied. He came to the house first brought by Theresa late one evening. I recall the visit well.

Claudio was a smallish man, impeccable, slim and with an air of disquiet around him. Although his manner was cultured and pleasant, his eyes were hard and his mouth a thin line, a mouth which could well denote cruelty. "Please, my friend, Claudio, you meet him," said Theresa as she introduced him in her halting English. Chen was seated in a garden chair, white wicker, and he remained seated as Claudio took his hand with ceremony, bowing over it in a gesture of respect which was so exaggerated as to be obviously insincere. He was a man with an elevated opinion of himself, maybe justified, maybe not, his manners, though, were elaborate, and his command of the English language excellent.

We all drank tea together, although I had the distinct feeling he would have preferred Scotch, and made polite conversation. Then Chen suggested Ra'ab and I withdraw, he would like to see Claudio and Theresa alone together. This was a departure from his usual procedure and I have no idea what actually took place at that meeting. On this and all subsequent meetings alone with Claudio, Chen remained silent. But what did happen was that Claudio became like a lamb, like a convert almost in that he seemed to rely on and believe in Chen totally, and was constantly turning up at the flat to seek his advice on this, that, or the other. Claudio was a leader in political affairs in the country - and the politics were complicated and devious. No one knew whose throat was going to be cut next, they just hoped it would not be theirs. Elimination by a bullet in the back of the head was not uncommon. Chen was essentially straightforward, and it must have been difficult for him to deal with Claudio's inborn deviousness and suberterfuge, however, he did all he could for this man because he felt indebted to him and the debt had to be paid back more than in full. Chen often explained that he had no kharma on Earth, so if anything were not paid back now, the debt would fall to someone else in a later life. He never allowed a debt to accrue.

It took nearly two years to get payment from the publishers in Buenos Aires, they were masters of procrastination. In the end, exasperated beyond belief, Chen threatened to write to the Argentinian President, a threat which he carried out, and when the police arrived at the publishers' office – they paid. They were too astonished to do anything else! Threats were customary, commonplace one might say, but as often as not were never carried out; it was a threat, no more, so when a threat actually was acted upon it threw everyone involved into a state of panic. For us it was a helpful state and certainly a great relief to have the matter settled, to have what monies were owing, because now finally we were entirely independent.

The Spanish editions published in Argentina were somewhat sensational in appearance. Large sized paperbacks with bright covers and poor paper, they were nonetheless immensely popular. My Spanish is not fluent enough for me to be able to make a fair criticism of the translations. There was, however, a well known firm in Spain, Destino, publishing different translations, and these books are beautifully produced. I have them still. There was never any problem with payments or any disagreement with the publisher in Spain, quite the contrary in fact.

It must have been when we were in Montevideo that another film offer was made and rejected. There had been one earlier on for 'The Third Eye,' but Chen was not interested, believing it would not convey the same message as his book, and I am sure he was right. Occasionally a film can be as good as a book, but not this kind of book done by that kind of filmmaker. What makes me sure the second offer occurred at that time was a conversation I remember having with Theresa, who had decided to make a friend of me and would invite me to lunch or tea from time to time. Her taste was flamboyant, but she had the means to execute it in the best possible way, and to visit her was almost to enter an extravagantly contrived theatrical set. Her ideas were somewhat weird, veering off from real life in all directions, and her interest in the occult, I am afraid, came under that heading; she was mainly interested because of her disinterest in reality, not necessarily from a desire to become more Aware. But she was, despite that, a good companion if not taken too seriously, talkative and lively, cultured and sensitive to social graces, and one could depend on her always to be tactful and kind.

This day I am remembering, the day we had the conversation about the film, was midsummer, probably around the second Christmas we were there. Her flat was airy, it boasted large casement windows which, when opened wide, caused a refreshing breeze to gently flow through the place. I liked going there, being ensconced in one of her huge enveloping chairs or lounging on the claw-footed sofa with eagle heads for arms, stacked with elaborate cushions covered in vibrant purple, gold and crimson silks and damasks, ancient needlepoint, and remnants of fine old carpets. The black silk curtains were draped and hanging in place of doors, defining the different areas of the large, rambling space, and they trailed on the marbled floors, partially looped back with tasseled dark green silk cords. They billowed and moved gently as the breeze took them. It imparted a delusional but convincing feeling of coolness.

We had just returned from a shopping spree, Theresa and I. She favoured an establishment situated on one of the wide boulevards of the city, a smart area away from the busier business district, where she liked to pick up clothes and accessories imported from Europe, mostly from France and Italy. I had managed to sidestep her buying a gift for me with difficulty, because she liked to be generous, but there was no dissuading her from buying a cream coloured silk scarf for Chen.

"You think he like?" she enquired, seating herself cross-legged on an oversized floor cushion.

"Yes, I should think so, they give scarves in Tibet, you know, when they visit each other," I told her, as I idly wondered if she was truly comfortable sitting cross-legged or if it was a pose, something she had adopted for meditation because that was how it was done in the East where they sat like that routinely. As if sitting cross-legged on the floor was mandatory for meditation! Her maid entered noiselessly on bare feet, and placed a tray with tall glasses of iced tea on the low japanned table set between us.

"Tell me, Amapola, about this film. The lama talk about it yesterday, but I don't ask more. It be done?" (Amapola was the nickname the translator had used in the books, feeling that the Spanish word for Buttercup was ugly).

"No, no, he won't allow it." I replied. "He doesn't like the fact that they want to suggest a homosexual relationship between him and his Guide, the Lama Mingyar Dondup."

"Dios mio, no, no, por supuesto, no, no!" She was adamant in her disgust. "These film people, que horrible, que feo, they are evil. How they think the lama be so wicked?" Theresa was aghast. I was taken aback by her reaction.

"Theresa, it's not that he sees it as wicked, or sees the film people as evil, or anything like that. It's just that it wasn't so, it wasn't a homosexual thing, it was a loving and caring situation between teacher and student. That's all, that's what it was, that's why it was so beautiful and enduring, " I told her. "It would be misleading to put a wrong interpretation on it, it would make his story quite different, wouldn't it?"

She put her glass down on the tray while staring at me in disbelief. "The lama, he have nothing against homosexuals? But they evil men!! They do terrible things to small boys. Amapola, I do not believe you, you say it wrong!"

"Well, you should talk to him about it, but until you do it's ridiculous to say they 'do terrible things to small boys.'" I told her. "You are thinking of paedophiles. They are the ones who 'do terrible things,' as you put it. But a paedophile, well, they can be hetersexual, bi-sexual or anything else, not just homosexual. Homosexuals are like everyone else except that they deviate sexually from what we consider as normal. But normal only means the majority, after all." I could see she was genuinely upset, but her attitude was widespread at that time. She remained silent and introspective. I had touched a sensitive nerve. She did, in fact, bring the subject up with Chen later, but her feeling around this may have had a lot to do with her gradual cooling – while Claudio became more and more trusting and believing – that and the fact that Chen did not quite fit the image of him that she had created in her mind. She had expected something like the cult groups of today. She was ready to sit at his feet and be taught Eastern postures in the hopes of gaining esoteric knowledge and awareness. She was not ready for self-reliance, and his straightforward, commonsense approach must have been a disillusionment to her.

Coincidental with the payment of monies due from Buenos Aires, the club began to die a natural death. It was never something suited to Chen's way of life or his belief, and from the beginning he had said it would not be permanent; it was a necessary means to an end, and he fulfilled his part of the bargain in an exemplary manner. We remained in touch with the core members, but moved to a different apartment, much smaller and in the heart of the city, and while we were living there he completed another book. Now that the group was disbanded, he felt freer and managed to get out more during the time he was dictating the book. Writing can be a very intense activity, and the writer needs a change of scenery to regenerate. During the writing of the book he was able to fulfil that particular need.

As always, I was transcribing his dictation. By this time we had worked together for a number of years, even so I never failed to be astonished at how he could dictate so evenly, clearly, and then at the end of the cassette he would stop perhaps in mid-sentence, only to start again the next day at the selfsame spot. While in no way an expert on brain function, I have to say that his brain appeared to function on an entirely different level from normal. This was apparent all the time, and one came to take it for granted. But looking back, and now able to compare it with people around me at present, it was truly remarkable, not only his genius, but that fact that he was able to converse with simple people entirely on their level without ever confusing them or talking down to them, in fact he seemed to prefer simple people, perhaps finding them more genuine.

With the book and the club behind him, it was time to make plans to return to Canada. I was not happy. I had enjoyed Montevideo, and the thought of returning filled me with gloom and reluctance. In my heart I knew it was inevitable, all the same I put up considerable resistance. In the end, with great understanding of the situation, Chen suggested that if I did not settle down in Canada after a year he would do what he could to facilitate my return to Montevideo. I am sure he meant it, but I am equally sure he knew it would not materialize. It did, though, achieve the end result of a peaceful departure from Montevideo.

The return journey to North America was entirely unlike the one going out. Physically it was the same thing back to front, the same shipping line, much the same ports of call, but there the similarity ended. The ship on the return journey was carrying the full complement of passengers, putting an entirely different picture on the voyage. The other people were a group of retired North Americans who, having finally escaped the gilded slavery of the work force, were intent on seeing the world by freighter. It is no doubt a very good way to see it, but they were tourists, not travellers. They filled their days with games; deck games, lounge games, the game of doing each port of call to the utmost, shopping and seeing. They were frenzied in their efforts to have fun, and appeared to have regressed to their high school days in their happiness at being released from work. I think we did our best to be polite, but very soon the conversation dried up. There was nothing to say, we did not want to join in their fun and would not have known how to, in any case, so we were written off as being dull and beyond comprehension.

It meant that we kept largely to our staterooms, and that had an interesting outcome. We spent time with tarot cards, the crystal, and discussions about occult matters. These things were, of course, our life, especially Chen's, but normally we did not have time to have such deep personal discussions because we were focussed on others, the research, the books, answering queries and attempting to help. Also, it is very possible that Chen's abilities were more heightened as we were actually on the ocean, almost a part of that majestic, unforgiving element. The higher vibrational senses of occultism must have flowed with greater ease and familiarily.

He told me many things on that voyage, not only to do with my own life, but things in general to do with the planet at present, in the past and in the future. He used his crystal extensively, focussing the third eye as he gazed into it, receiving pictures, impressions and scenes, sometimes quite randomly and unexpectedly. When a scryer, or crystal gazer, gets in contact, it is as if he or she 'falls' into the scene presented, they are actually there in another dimension, and should never be disturbed. They are quite definitely out of themselves, they are operating in a different time.

There were three things he told me, amongst the many, that stuck in my mind because I found them at the time difficult to believe, and just put them on hold until such time as they might, possibly, become more credible. They have, actually, all come to pass. It was not that I doubted his ability, it was simply that these three things seemed so very improbable. But life can and does take unexpected twists and turns. That is what makes it an adventure.

It was when we docked at New York and left the ship, having to manoeuvre the docks and the seemingly endless formalities that Chen first began to use a wheel chair. His back had been troublesome and he felt unable to walk and stand around, as one has to in such situations, so the wheelchair offered great relief, and when we were more or less settled again in Canada he purchased one. From New York we travelled back to Ontario, and this time put up at a rather sleezy hotel, quite curious, never a dull moment you might say, with all the comings and goings and carryings-on of a varied clientele. Chen liked being around the man in the street, the common man, and these certainly were that, or perhaps 'the man in the tavern' would be a more apt description. This hotel was on the Niagara Parkway at a place called Prescott. It was a temporary arrangement that strung out much longer than intended, but in time we were moving again, this time to New Brunswick.

Although there was a tremendous amount of fog in St. John, where we decided to live, the general atmosphere was much more pleasant than we had ever found Ontario to be. The people initially seemed unfriendly, but when they got to know you, they opened up. There was a natural reserve, which in the longrun is a good thing, reminiscent of the Scots and their caution of strangers. It was a fishing town, hilly and healthy. We stayed at another hotel for a time, this one with the impressive name of 'The Admiral Beatty,' and from there we found an apartment on a hill overlooking the sea, where we remained for a few months. Our belongings were minimal, as they always had been, but we had what was necessary for working. Although New Brunswick was not a bad place, in fact a pleasant place in many ways, it was too cut off for Chen. He felt he was wasting time, he had the pressing urgency to be where things were moving, a centre. So, once again we packed up and were off, this time to Montreal.

Of all the places I have lived in Canada, I found Montreal the most compatible. In my experience of Canadians I have found them, for the most part, to be astonishingly, almost frighteningly, law-abiding. One could reason that this phenomenon is due to fear, but in the case of Canadians I truly believe it is because they, as a nation, like to please, they hate to upset others, they are thoroughly nice people. If, for instance, someone is wanting to cross the street at dead of night, and there is no vehicle within sight or sound, they will solemnly wait until the walk sign comes on, with the little lit-up white person striding along, and then, and only then, will they cross the street, looking neither to left or right because they know the street is clear, the sign told them so. And besides, they are so law-abiding no one could possibly be running a red light so it is perfectly safe to cross the street as soon as the walk sign lights up. But there is always an exception to any rule, and that exception, in my experience, was Montreal.

I found a delightful piquancy to Montreal entirely lacking elsewhere in Canada. There were good concerts, people were interested in literature, antiques, art at a time when there was precious little anywhere else in the country. Culture was a natural part of the place, not something that people did because they thought they should be cultured. Enjoyment of life, 'joie de vivre,' was natural, too. They seemed to look at life in a different way, they did not really try so hard to be nice, they liked to have a good time. We lived exactly the same kind of life in Montreal as anywhere else, that is, not mixing, living a reclusive life on the whole, but one still picks up an atmosphere and either thrives or subsides on it. I thrived on Montreal.

It must have been 1968 or '69 when we moved there. For once, I am more or less sure of the date because we rented an apartment in Habitat. Habitat had been built for Expo in 1967, and now found itself almost empty. The rents had been astronomically high during Expo, and no one wanted to pay that amount of money for the pleasure of living there once Expo was over and done with. What was not generally realised was that Habitat had been put in the hands of Central Mortgage and Housing, a government run agency, and the rents had dropped to a reasonable rate. Our apartment was a large one on the upper levels of Habitat, and situated at the far end with a marvellous view up river and of any shipping coming down. It was, in fact, something like the deck of a ship, and unique in many ways. Chen kept a coloured index of flags of the world pinned over his bed; any ship coming in view was identified by its flag right away.

The architect responsible for designing and building Habitat was Jewish and familiar with similar structures in the Middle East, but it was something of a wonder at that time in Canada. The apartments were placed in odd juxtaposition, never exactly alongside or directly above or below each other, and therefore individual and separate. They were not uniform in interior layout; some were on one level only, others on two, in some the bedrooms were on the upper level, in others they were on the lower. Each unit had been prefabricated to design and then dropped into place by huge cranes as the building progressed. The whole place was contructed in concrete. There were glass covered walkways, or streets, all around the building, and elevators which were reached by traversing the walkways. There was a central lobby which was manned by officers of the Corps of Commissionaires, and we found them very pleasant and helpful.

When we first lived there there was a limousine at the disposal of tenants, doing runs back and forth to downtown, dropping us at Birks in the centre of the city, and picking us up there on the return journey. Whenever I went downtown there were seldom any others tenants wishing to go at the same time, so I rode in the back of the limousine in state. When I was ready to go home, I called up and the car came to get me. In any case, only about four other apartments were occupied initially, but as the place filled up, the limousine was replaced by a bus running at set times only, but still free of charge. I unashamedly enjoyed it all. Ra'ab really enjoyed it, too, although was always reluctant to admit to a liking for any kind of luxury.

Chen found the place very suitable for several reasons – it was right on the water, the rooms and corridors were large and easy to manouevre by wheelchair (he had an electric chair by now, a Swiss made machine and very dependable), it was a new concept in housing for this part of the world, and it was progressive. It was close to downtown, but there was still lots of parkland to explore, and the many outstanding Expo pavilions which still were open, or some of them, in the summer months. He did not, and never did, enjoy luxury or fuss of any kind. But he was practical. He was disabled, and knew his body was already worn out, although he was not yet quite ready to give it up, so it was easier to live in comfortable surroundings where it was quiet and spacious. He liked to drive around the streets of Habitat in the wheelchair, which was possible even in the winter because the glass covered streets were heated. He enjoyed the odd encounter with the people in charge of running the place, and I remember one such encounter very well.

I nearly always accompanied him when he went out. He had suffered several brief black-outs recently, over in a matter of seconds almost, but he was loathe to black-out while driving the wheelchair, or in a place where some well-intentioned person might send for an ambulance. So I went with him on foot, although later on I acquired a bicycle and we covered much greater distances together.

This particular day we were about to take the elevator up to the top floor after a walk around the grounds, and an extensive and fascinating talk to the Swiss head gardener, or landscaper, as he probably would have preferred to be known. Chen had driven slowly, allowing me to keep up with him - this was prior to the bicycle - and we had already been out for an hour or so, and were feeling chilled by this time. As we waited for the elevator, a rotund little figure appeared around the corner, also heading for the elevator. We recognised him as M. Marchand, the representative of Central Mortgage and Housing, who was usually around the place, doing who-knows-what, but having his own little office close to the grocery store on the lower level. He was a bustling type of individual, with a permanent smile on his round, bespectacled face, and a habit of running his hand over his bald pate, seemingly to make sure every non-existent hair was in place. He spoke English with a very marked French-Canadian accent, but with such rapidity, constantly running off track, that it was never easy to follow his meaning. That was the main reason Chen did his best to avoid him. At this point, however, we were caught, and there was no escape.

"Ah, well, well, how are you, doctor? A beautiful day, no? Cold, um, perhaps, but still so beautiful, so beautiful." He beamed and rubbed his head energetically. "And the beautiful young lady, well, I hope, yes, yes, so nice to be young and beautiful." He was a pain, although unintentionally funny sometimes. We piled into the elevator together, subjected to his running commentary, but as soon as the door closed, shutting us all in and with no one else to hear, he became quieter and almost conspiratorial. Bending over Chen's chair, speaking close to his ear in a hushed voice, he said, "I would like to show you a very special little place here at Habitat, doctor, you like that, eh?"

Chen regarded him silently for a moment, then to my great surprise he nodded and replied, "Yes, M. Marchand, I would like that very much."

The little man continued smiling, and rubbed his hands together. "Well, now we send the young lady home, no? This is for men only, ha, ha." He giggled at his own remark, then seeing my ill-disguised look of boredom, he added, "You wouldn't be interested, no, no, this is business only, not for lovely ladies."

The elevator door opened at the upper level, and Chen looked at me with the merest wink. "All right, I'll see you soon, I expect Ra'ab has tea ready for us," he said as I stepped out, leaving them to it.

M. Marchand pushed the button after my exit and they returned to the concourse level. He got out first and Chen followed him. As he walked along beside the wheelchair he got out a large bunch of keys, which he jangled as they went. It seemed to be an accompaniment to his endless conversation. "Ah, here we are," he announced as they arrived at one of the more secluded apartments, round the back of two others which occupied the best place on the concourse. He fitted the key, turned it and pushed open the door, beckoning for Chen to follow. They found themselves in what Chen later described as a 'very sumptious place,' fitted out like something one might see illustrated in an exclusive magazine. The carpet was so thick that the wheelchair made heavy going of it. There was a sideboard 'filled with bottles of alcohol,' according to Chen, comfortable chairs, paintings on the walls. It felt as if it was used. M. Marchand took an easy chair and allowed Chen a moment to look around.

"So, doctor, you like this place, eh?" he enquired.

Chen took his time. "No, I can't say I do. It has a very strange atmosphere. A lot of people come here, don't they? And I can make one guess as to why they come."

"Well, you may be right, we are men of the world, aren't we, doctor. We know what makes the world go round. Nothing wrong with that, nothing wrong at all." M. Marchand sniggered. "The oldest profession of all, you could say, and perhaps – yes, just perhaps – the most necessary. Doctor, you and I, we know about the world. Men must be kept happy, men have to make decisions, big decisions, and they need to be kept happy so they can make good decisions. But – and I assure you of this – only the most important men come here, I assure you, oh yes, only the best. Highly placed men, wealthy men. And only the most exclusive, mature ladies, for that matter, to entertain them."

"I see," said Chen, "But I wonder why you have invited me here?"

"Why? My dear doctor, can you not guess? Yes, surely you can! As I say, we have only the most exclusive ladies, and I wonder, I just wonder, if your secretary - - - " he trailed off, passing his hand over his head as he did so.

"My secretary? No, you are mistaken, M. Marchand." Chen laughed. "Mrs. Rouse is a member of my family. She's no more a secretary than she's a prostitute."

"Oh dear me, please not to use that dreadful word!" M. Marchand extracted a handkerchief from his pocket and held it to his nose, as though the shock was too much for him. "These are not ladies of the night, these are ladies of the highest, how do you say? calibre? Is that the right word? I think so. Calibre. Of course I wouldn't think of offending, no, no. But the money

– well, the money. We all need it, you know, and – " rubbing his finger and thumb together, and with a sly wink, "well, the money, it is considerable, I assure you. The young lady, I don't for a moment suggest she is a lady of the night, nothing like that. Here we are elegant, exclusive. Please, doctor," he looked pained as spoke, "please don't use that vulgar word 'prostitute' again. This is entirely different."

Chen smiled. "It may be a vulgar word, but it comes to the same thing. You need prostitutes. But I am afraid you are assuming too much. No, Mrs. Rouse would not be interested. And now I have to get home, my wife has tea waiting." He steered his wheelchair towards the door. M. Marchand appeared undaunted. He shrugged, as only a French-Canadian can, indicating that that was that, too bad if the other was not interested, it was his loss. But he took the refusal in good part. As he locked the door, he half turned to Chen and said, "Just between ourselves, of course, doctor, just between ourselves. No matter, I will still make sure you are looked after at Habitat. It lies in my hands, you know." His meaning was clear.

"Of course, M. Marchand. Just between ourselves, have no fear. And you are right, we all need money. You get yours one way, I get mine another, and we won't interfere with each other. Now, if you will be good enough to send for the elevator, thank you. Good afternoon."

When I heard the story, I just wondered if perhaps, after all, I had missed my vocation!! It was a standing joke between us for a long time afterwards, and proved that perhaps one does not ever see oneself as others might see you – especially in Montreal

* * *

The time we spent in Montreal proved to be a hiatus in writing for Chen. There were different reasons for this. One may have been that it was simply necessary to have a pause. Another was that with his electric Swiss-made wheelchair and my bicycle we covered distances and saw things we might not otherwise have seen, so we spent a good deal of time on that, on going out and seeing things of interest. Sunday morning early was our favourite time to go to old Montreal. There were lovely and interesting buildings, cobbled streets, fascinating names and odd corners, and there were few people around that early, which was a bonus. There was a large Rampa following in Montreal, he was easily recognizable, so a deserted street was always welcome. During the weekdays we often went over the bridge from Habitat to the Expo site. Here again, it was pretty much deserted except at weekends in the summer, but there was still an enormous amount to see; the pavilions erected by countries the world over were still there, still open sometimes, and many were quite lovely. And, of course, there was always the shipping to watch.

And yet another and more serious reason for his rest from writing was that Ra'ab experienced a prolonged episode of manic depression. The illness was generally under control, and who knows what caused it to recur in full force, but it did. Montreal and its vibrancy may have sparked an upsurge. Whatever it was, it began with a period of manic behaviour, which I find as disquieting as the low period of depression that follows. It was the start of a difficult period for us all and there were times when I would gladly have left and found a job, any job, any small place to live on my own, just to get away.

I was also troubled because of a new direction Chen seemed to be taking. For years he had shunned all publicity, a wise stance for various reasons, not the least being that in this way no one knew him, no one had met him, no one could truthfully make a statement about him, no one could say that he was this, that or the other because he remained isolated from the public eye. He wrote his books, and the time and effort that went into that was immense. He could complete a book quickly, but it had already been well thought out in his mind, and when he came to dictate it was always under tremendous pressure. The books, then, were one thing, but he felt that he as a person was of no interest, he was private and he fiercely guarded his privacy, but all of a sudden he agreed to a television interview. I felt strongly that television was not the kind of advertising he needed or should use, I felt it cheapened his image, his serious readers would be gravely disillusioned, I thought, and I told him how I felt.

Looking back with hindsight, he probably had his own good reasons, but at the time I could see no reason good enough for his peristence, I could only guess. It caused a serious rift between us. He told me pointedly that a chain is only as strong as its weakest link. I was angry, hurt and disappointed. I had been supportive through thick and thin and still was, and to be classified as the weakest link was unjustified. But when I suggested any change in our living arangements - that I move out and live alone, he displayed alarm, heart problems, anything to make me stay. We got through it, of course, and stayed together for many more years, almost to the end of his life. Looking at the painting now and seeing things more dispassionately, I believe he did have his good reasons and that my alarm was unjustified, even though at the time I was convinced I was right.

During that period I spent a good deal of time in antique shops, boutiques, book shops, and art galleries. The museum on Sherbrooke Street in Montreal was also the art gallery and had a system of allowing people to rent paintings. I went in for that for a time, not the Old Masters, they were not rentable, but nevertheless there were reasonably good paintings available for one to take home for a few weeks. When in the museum I often would sit and contemplate an El Greco painting which hung in an alcove. I have no idea if it is still there, but the peaceful, uplifting vibrations emanating from that painting were remarkable, almost hypnotic. Whether it was the work itself or the collective homage of the hundreds of viewers who had gazed on it over the years, I cannot say, but it existed and it eased one's mind. For another diversion I sometimes had a rendezvous with a rather nice man who worked in one of the art galleries I visited, but then I found out he was married and an alcoholic, so not the best choice in the world!

After a few years Montreal began to pall and it was time for another move. This time we crossed the entire continent to the West coast, and it was here in Vancouver that Chen's illnesses took a hold and he entered the final phase of his life.

CHAPTER NINE

My magic painting is practically finished now. The story is nearly told, but the ending is as strange as the beginning. I do not understand fully what happened when I left Chen. Perhaps when I complete this life I will be able to understand, in fact I am sure I will, but for now, with only limited vision, I believe that I did what I had to do, I fulfilled my commitment to him, and it was simply that time had run out. But I am running on ahead of myself, I am not quite there yet, my story is not quite finished, the picture is not complete in all its details.

Chen and I had visited Vancouver once several years before we went to live there. We went as well to Victoria on Vancouver Island for a very brief visit, just a matter of days. We had planned to stay at the Empress Hotel in Victoria, and the Vancouver Hotel in Vancouver, but when we arrived he refused to enter either. They reminded him of British hotels, one in particular in India where he had been refused admission on the grounds that he was coloured, a native. He had been deeply insulted. He was an intensely sensitive and proud man.

As it happens, I do not believe we missed anything at all by bypassing those two hotels. I seem to remember us putting up at small, modest places which were much nicer. Victoria for Chen was not attractive, it was too British, too staid, too backwards-looking, entrenched in a sort of pseudo- tradition more British than the British, and he was a man of the future. It was not the place for him. Vancouver, too, at the time we first visited was very conservative, very unaccepting of new thought, but by the time we went to live there it was beginning to change.

It would be in the 70's that we moved from Montreal to Vancouver. I had by that time acquired one or two good pieces of furniture in old Montreal which I had no wish to leave behind. Although the Rampa's disliked owning material things, Chen understood my love of old objects, something which sustains me in a world I sometimes find unbearable, and never tried to dissuade me from acquisitions, nor from hauling those pieces right across the continent, which I did. And they survived, they still survive!

Even though they disliked owning things, it would not be correct to say that Chen and Ra'ab did not shop. They did, but they seldom kept what they bought. What they bought was used and then circulated, given away to people who would appreciate it or who needed it, so when we moved, they moved with very little, the rest was left for someone else to use, and essentials, such as beds, were purchased at the next home. For Chen the monetary value was unimportant, it literally meant nothing. Monetary value to him was something artificial which had been put in place by the merchants and did not at all represent the real value. He had very little to do with money; Ra'ab was the one who handled it, who went to the bank, who talked to the people who took care of money in banks. He knew what was going on, of course, but he seldom actually handled money.

His shopping amounted to things for his work which I have already mentioned, but also things for hobbies, and books, clocks, watches. At one time he possessed some of the most beautiful and intricate watches and clocks I have ever seen, antique watches, old French and Swiss watches exquisitely decorated, perfect timekeepers, hour repeaters and even minute repeaters. He studied them, he studied their construction, he kept them for a while, and then he gave them away.

As his health deteriorated he bought and became very interested in aids for invalids. This was an ongoing state of affairs for a number of years, and I knew the inside of hospital equipment businesses in Vancouver, and later Calgary, intimately; I was the one who went to buy or exchange things he had seen in catalogues, Ra'ab had discussed on the telephone, and then he obtained to test, not necessarily for his own comfort but for interest in the comfort of others in the same plight as he was in, or worse – in the plight of disabled people, to acquaint himself better with their lives.

He relentlessly wrote strong letters to city officials demanding ramps on sidewalks for wheelchairs. When he first started using a wheelchair outside, it was dreadfully difficult to cross streets and alleyways because there were absolutely no ramps anywhere. One seldom encountered a person in a wheelchair in those days, they stayed indoors or on balconies or yards, and it was curious how a person in a wheelchair then, such as Chen, caused embarrassment to the fit and able. They turned away, they avoided us. Now, there are ramps everywhere, there are people in wheelchairs everywhere, and Chen was largely responsible for it. He never gave up writing to influential people on the issue of ramps and easy access for invalids, and he wrote letters which were hard to ignore.

When we arrived in Vancouver we rented an apartment on an upper floor of a large hotel in an area known as the West End, and we stayed in that apartment the whole time we lived in the city. It overlooked English Bay and the view was pleasant for Chen who by that time was spending an ever increasing amount of time in bed. There were regular hotel rooms on the lower floors, and the arrangement worked well for us in that we had the best of both worlds - the convenience of a hotel but the privacy of our own apartment.

It was largely in the West End that Chen and I traversed the streets with the wheelchair, but only at quiet times because we soon discovered that he was extremely well known in Vancouver. The West End was not nearly so busy as it is now, but even so there were few really quiet times on the streets. Chen got so discouraged by this that when fans rushed up to him saying, "Oh Dr. Rampa! It can't be Lobsang Rampa!" he would look amazed, and say in a gruff voice, "Lobsang Who? Never heard of the fellow." and take off as fast as the wheelchair would carry him. I am sure he fooled no one, but at least they got the message, and I got the exercise sprinting along after him.

Vancouver was, and is, a beautiful city and has a mild climate. Now, as I write, it is growing by leaps and bounds, everywhere there are huge skyscrapers, every available bit of land is being utilized and prices are soaring. Back in the 70's it was far more pleasant, but now the modest citizens who have lived here for years are being displaced. It is too costly for them, they are having to move out and are being replaced by wealth and all that goes along with it.

Even in the 70's, though, to a sensitive there was an overwhelming aura of discontent in Vancouver. There were constant strikes, rumblings of unrest sparked by those who like to create chaos by working on the less literate sectors of a society. It is still a discontented place in spite of, or perhaps because of, the wealth, the play, the excesses. I knew from the start that Vancouver would be as temporary as any other place we had lived, perhaps more so, and the reason we stayed as long as we did was because of Chen's disabilities, particularly with walking. It began in earnest the day he fell down and was completely unable to move, and even while keeping perfectly still was clearly in great pain. We waited an hour or so, trying to relax his muscles by any means possible, but at last decided we had to get medical help. This was a serious problem with his spine.

At the bottom of the street there was a medical clinic. It was a busy place, and the several doctors who worked there were seeing people every fifteen minutes or so. One of the major services they provided was to check the prostitutes regularly for disease. However, we managed to get one of the doctors to come to the apartment. He was an immensely tall man, reluctant to be taken from his practice, but he took one look at Chen, then gave him a large shot of Demerol. "That should do it," he said, as he snapped his bag shut. "I'll leave you some more in case you need it." It did indeed "do it," and within a short time we were able to get Chen up and into his bed.

People used to write wondering why it was that he could not control his pain and illnesses. My answer is that to a large extent he did. By the laws of nature he would have lived perhaps ten or fifteen years less than he actually did. During the early years of our time together he had great control, and surmounted much physical pain and disability, but as time went on it became increasingly difficult.

As soon as he recovered a little from that spinal attack, he was thinking again of moving. We still had two Siamese cats, and to find an apartment in Vancouver accepting of animals at that time was virtually impossible. In the hotel we were lucky; it was a different arrangement from normal regarding animals, perhaps based on temporary residence, so we were able to have the cats in the apartment with no trouble, but living there was proving too expensive. We had to think of somewhere other than Vancouver. I am not sure now what made him think of Calgary in Alberta, but he did, and we moved there sight unseen. It was a unique move for us because we were not on, or even near, the water. It turned out to be Chen's last move.

Calgary was just taking off with the oil boom, but at the time we arrived there were still plenty of vacant apartments. The rents were reasonable, and no one minded cats or dogs or anything else, they just wanted to rent their places. After Vancouver, with its splendid mountains, ocean, trees and gardens, Calgary seemed arid and ugly. The climate was difficult, too, extreme cold and extreme heat, but at least it had the saving grace of the Chinook's, those warm winds that blow from time to time in the icy winter months, bringing a few days respite from the bitter cold, when ice melts and ear muffs can be dispensed with. In time, as we got to know Calgary and Calgarians it took on a much better feeling. On the whole, we were contented there until Chen's health took a sharp downward spiral, and we began to have a regular attending physician.

He needed someone near at hand all the time, and I started to stay with him at night, taking my mattress from my room next door to his and laying it down on the floor beside his bed. He would often settle down for the night very early, sometimes around 5 p.m., and might waken several times during the night for medication, a cup of tea, or just a chat – companionship.

I have always gone to bed early, and seem to need more hours of sleep than most people, but on his very early nights I would prop myself up with pillows against the wall on my mattress and work on my needlepoint for a few hours. I actually found those hours extremely satisfactory. By his breathing pattern I would know he was out of the body and I must be quiet, make no sudden movements that might bring him back sharply. I stitched away, quiet as a mouse, composing my patterns and colours, concentrated completely on my work. It was a hobby one could engage in in that situation much more easily than, say, painting, and I became reasonably skilled at it. I loved doing it.

Anyone who has taken care of a terminally ill patient will know that it is not easy. One has to make the patient as comfortable as possible without unnecessarily prolonging life, but the natural instinct we have is to keep the patient alive at all costs, not for the patient who is dying anyway and does not need the process strung out any longer than necessary, but for ourselves. We hate to see them declining, becoming weaker, losing control, we hate the thought that soon they will no longer be with us.

With Chen, however, I think it was easier than with most people at the end of their lives. For one thing, he knew the Other Side of death, he had no fear, it was only a journey. We openly discussed his death, in fact we had always talked about death and dying as part of life. He did prolong things perhaps longer than he need have done, and he did fight his illnesses and disabilities, perhaps all the time hoping there was more he could comprehend about the human condition that would be of value to those in the astral observing the Earth.

As the months went by he appeared to me to lose his powers. He insisted on continuing to write, but his last books were nothing like the former ones. They were full of repetition, and he was not pleased when I pointed this out to him. I felt he would lose his audience, they would not appreciate his earlier work so much if he continued to write when he was visibly failing.

The dynamics in our family changed, too. He had always been the one in control. Ra'ab and I were in his charge and he was the Master. Ra'ab had always resented that. She was of a type who liked to be in charge, and had no concept that often it is the one behind the throne who has the real power. She had always been in a way jealous of Chen's success because she liked the limelight. One has to remember that he was not the man she married, even the body of her husband, Cyril Hoskins, had been replaced molecule by molecule over the years and now was completely Chen's own body. It is more than likely that her husband was a much weaker character and needed a woman like Ra'ab to dominate him, but Chen was certainly not one to be dominated. He ruled with wisdom and compassion. He allowed complete freedom in some things, but in others – he led us.

As he weakened so Ra'ab strengthened. I was not happy with the new regime, but it was prudent for me to go along with things, cause no ripples, we had a sick man to care for and that was the major concern. I became even less happy when Ra'ab decided to start writing. In my opinion, that would detract even more from Chen's earlier and best works, and I knew her motivation was for fame, and perhaps to ensure a living for herself after he had died. You could argue that there was nothing wrong with that, but I guarded Chen's reputation with perhaps a little too much care, and to me it was distasteful. She saw a brighter future for herself through Chen, perhaps, but without his presence. I felt our whole structure was crumbling.

It came to a head after many months. We had settled down early for the night, but I had a light shining on my canvas and was working on it when I felt Chen watching me. I looked up and asked if he was all right.

"Yes," he said, "I'm just watching you." He paused, then went on, his voice weaker now than it used to be, but still firm, "Buttercup, I want you to stay with Ra'ab when I'm gone."

My fingers continued to work, and I bent my head over the canvas again. I did not dare or want to meet his eyes.

Eventually I said, "No, Chen, I'm sorry I can't. She wouldn't want it anyway."

"It's for your own good, you know. What would you do otherwise?" he asked.

Chen and I often made light of troubling things just to put them in perspective, so I said, half jokingly, and looking him straight in the face, "Chen, what are you thinking of? You say you need me around to make life lighter, why do you expect me to stay when you are not around?"

"She'll be better when I'm not around."

"That's nonsense, Chen, you know it is!" The thought of living with Ra'ab alone filled me with dread. I knew I would be shredded to bits in a matter of days. If anyone stayed with her it would have to be someone much tougher than I could ever be.

"If you stay with her, you'll get my money when she dies, and she won't live that long," he said firmly.

I could scarcely believe what I was hearing. I put my work down and stared at him, at this man who knew me inside out, this man who I had cared for exclusively for over twenty years, with whom I had an enviable rapport and who had shown love and deep friendship which I had returned in full, unconditionally. This man was trying to bribe me! He was trying to persuade me to take on a task he knew I could not do by offering me money! He was adding insult to injury.

"I'm not here for your money. I don't care about your money, I don't want it!" I knew only too well that he must not be upset in his state of health, yet I had to be honest with him.

What had happened? Was this really Chen saying these things? It could not be, I reasoned, he must already have left for the Heavenly Fields and this was some other person, someone who knew nothing about me. Chen knew me so well, so very well, he knew I could never be approached on that level. He knew, also, I could never stay alone with Ra'ab. He knew my reaction would be totally negative.

He lay down and turned over, his back to me. And then he said, "You don't want my money after I've worked so hard for your future? I was even going to have a film made so you would be secure. But if you don't want it - well, now its different."

I made no reply. There was nothing to say because he was only trying another tactic. It saddened me that he felt he had to do that, that we had come to this.

As I write twenty-five years later and see things in a different light, it is entirely possible that he was actually deeply concerned for my financial wellbeing. He, who had known poverty, deprivation and starvation, knew also that I had been sheltered all my life and had no real experience of poverty or the battle of the work place. Yet, at the time, all I saw was lack of understanding, insult and coercion. And if he was so concerned why not simply provide for me without making conditions?

Whatever the truth, I was anguished. I knew absolutely clearly – as we do in times of great stress sometimes – that I had to leave, I had to leave now, immediately, no matter that he was ill, I had to leave so he and Ra'ab would know I was not prepared to stay after he died. It was not a case of walking away from responsibilities – I was being sent away, forced away, one could say. I had to be 'up front' so they would know I had no intention of staying when Chen had gone. I knew they could get a nurse to take over most of the care I was giving.

Ultimately, it had to happen, it was in the cards that I would not be with him when he died, and so it transpired. What follows is very strange and was an uncanny experience, even more so than my first encounter with him.

As soon as I made the decision to leave, it was as though I was taken over by some higher force, and I assumed it was my own Overself. Emotionally

I became numb, I felt nothing, I felt no grief, no reproach, no guilt, no joy, nothing. Physically, I lost my appetite and had to force myself to eat to keep alive, and to drink water. I literally was as a puppet going through the motions of life propelled from afar. Only if a person has had such an experience can they know what I am talking about. I went through the motions of gathering up my belongings and transferring myself to Vancouver, where I felt I would be able to get work in an antique shop. I had no force or energy of my own, I was, as I say, being propelled. If I had not already believed in the existence of an Overself, I would have been obliged to admit it as a reality at that time.

Ra'ab was more helpful to me than she had ever been. I am sure she had no more wish for us to be left alone together than I had. We had managed all those years because Chen was our motivation and stabilizer, but without him we were so dissimilar it would have been impossible and pointless. I had a little money of my own, but she made sure that I had enough to keep me going until I was established. She was pleasant. She was clearly thankful, almost jubilant, to see me depart, and perhaps she should not be blamed. I have sometimes wondered, however, if she fully realised that without my presence Chen would never have achieved what he did, and what he did was far, far greater than maybe either of us fully understood.

After being in Vancouver for ten days or so I recieved a telephone call from Ra'ab. Chen was inviting me home. I refused. Within two days I received a letter from him beginning, 'Dear Mrs. Rouse' and signed, 'T. Lobsang Rampa.' The letter was brief and to the point, disowning me completely. I felt nothing, but - I wondered why. I have no idea. Neither does it matter.

The last communication came just a few weeks later. It was a formal announcement of his death.

Of course, over the years I have wondered. What really happened? Time had run out and it may have been that I had to leave before he could be released from his body. I was the one keeping him on the Earth all those years, after all, I was his anchor and the anchor has to be lifted before the ship can embark on its voyage. It was time, past time, for his departure and sometimes things are not as they seem. I felt, and feel, no rancour. That was just the way it was.

His life was one of suffering but he achieved much. For most of his achievments he is not given credit, but in the end does it matter who gets the credit? All that matters is to get the job done. And that he did.

And me? Well, the three things he foretold on the journey back from Uruguay have all come to pass. The first was that I would not be there when he died. The second was that of my three children the youngest would be closest to me in old age. The third was that in the twilight years someone would come into my life who was just right. That someone is a constant delight; twenty-four years my junior, a homosexual man. We have lived under the same roof in perfect harmony, understanding and companionship for more than three years now. How many women of my age are so fortunate?

When I think of Chen, I have before me the image of him as he made those forecasts while looking at my hands. Then, taking my two hands in both his he smiled, that smile that lit his eyes, and said, "You'll be all right, Buttercup, you'll always be all right."

And so my painting is completed, my story of those years with the man who came to be known as Tuesday Lobsang Rampa is done. Now, quarter of a century on, the memory of this unique man is alive and with me still. There were ups and downs, good times and bad, but they were magical years, years lived almost in a different dimension from the mundane world we ordinarily inhabit.

His power, his love for all things, the depth of his personality surpassed understanding.

One day, perhaps sooner than we imagine, he will be acknowledged, understood and vindicated. I am sure of it. That we, the human race, will have the wisdom and spirituality to profit from his endeavours remains to be seen.

THE END

Lightning Source UK Ltd.
Milton Keynes UK
UKOW01f1915311017
311970UK00001B/302/P

9 781411 674325